Differentiated Instructional Strategies

Differentiated Instructional Strategies

One Size Doesn't Fit All

Gayle H. Gregory ♦ Carolyn Chapman

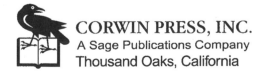

CORWIN PRESS, INC.
A Sage Publications Company
Thousand Oaks, California

For information:

Corwin Press, Inc.
A Sage Publications Company
2455 Teller Road
Thousand Oaks, California 91320
E-mail: order@corwinpress.com

Sage Publications Ltd.
6 Bonhill Street
London EC2A 4PU
United Kingdom

Sage Publications India Pvt. Ltd.
M-32 Market
Greater Kailash I
New Delhi 110 048 India

Printed in the United States of America

Library of Congress Cataloging-in-Publication Data

Gregory, Gayle.
    Differentiated instructional strategies: One size doesn't fit all /
by Gayle H. Gregory, Carolyn Chapman.
        p. cm.
    Includes bibliographical references and index.
    ISBN 0-7619-4550-4 (c) — ISBN 0-7619-4551-2 (p)
    1. Individualized instruction. 2. Cognitive styles in children. 3.
Mixed ability grouping in education.   I. Chapman, Carolyn. II. Title.
    LB1031 .G74 2002
    371.39′4—dc21   2001005120

This book is printed on acid-free paper.

        04   05   10   9

Illustrations by Tammy Kay Brunson, Thomson, GA 30824

Acquiring Editor:	Faye Zucker
Corwin Editorial Assistant:	Julia Parnell
Production Editor:	Diane S. Foster
Typesetter/Designer:	Larry K. Bramble
Indexer:	Will Ragsdale
Cover Designer:	Tracy E. Miller

Contents

1. Creating a Climate for Learning   **1**

Much has been researched and written about classroom climate and the need for a safe, nurturing environment with high challenge and low threat where all learners can thrive. This chapter explores ideas and strategies that can help teachers build this learning community so vital for success.

2. Knowing the Learner   **19**

Teachers must make every effort to know learners in order to meet their diverse needs. Just as clothing designers must know about the many fabrics and styles to create a garment to suit the wearer, so in classrooms we teachers must know about our learners so that we may find the strengths and uniqueness of each child. This chapter describes learning-styles theories, identifies multiple intelligences, and provides tools to help teachers identify their students' learning styles and preferences.

3. Assessing the Learner   **37**

Everyone needs feedback. Teachers and students need to exchange constant feedback to monitor progress and to adjust learning. It has been said that assessment drives the curriculum. Teachers need assessment tools to pre-assess to plan for learning as well as ongoing assessment tools to use during and after the learning process. Pre-assessment is essential for teachers to find out what students know, can do, and are interested in learning. If teachers use pre-assessment data when they are planning lessons, learners are not bored by repeating "history" or, conversely, lost with no frame of reference when the new learning is beyond their realm of experience. Suggestions and examples of effective pre-assessment tools are outlined as well as tools to use during and after the learning process. Ideas for grading are explored.

Acknowledgments

Two experienced educators developed this book: Gayle Gregory and Carolyn Chapman, both educational consultants. It responds to educators who have seen a need for an organized, practical, and comprehensive way to plan for classroom instruction that meets the needs of diverse learners in heterogeneous classrooms.

We are indebted to other professional educators for their work, writings, and examples and to family members for their love and support.

To our husbands, Joe and Jim, we express our thanks for understanding and encouragement in the long hours of writing, for ideas, listening, and editing.

We have been influenced and enlightened by outstanding professionals such as Pat Wolfe, Howard Gardner, Daniel Goleman, David Sousa, Bob Sylwester, Eric Jensen, Tony Gregorc, Bernice McCarthy, Carol Rolheiser, Bob Marzano, Jay McTighe, Carol Ann Tomlinson, Carol O'Connor, Pam Robbins, Rita King, Robin Fogarty, and Kay Burke, to mention a few.

Special thanks to friend and colleague Joanne Quinn, whose ongoing enthusiasm and support and good questions have helped clarify many issues in this book.

We dedicate this book to children everywhere in the hope that its content will help teachers meet their needs and empower learners to reach their potential and be the best they can be with joy, enthusiasm, creativity, and self-confidence.

The contributions of the following reviewers are gratefully acknowledged:

Maria Elena Reyes
Assistant Professor,
School of Education
University of Alaska
Fairbanks, AK

Kathleen Chamberlain
Assistant Professor of Education
Lycoming College
Williamsport, PA

Sarah Rees Edwards
Adjunct Professor
University of Arizona
Tucson, AZ

Steve Hutton
Principal
Beechwood Elementary School
Ft. Mitchell, KY

Mildred Murray-Ward
Chair, Department of Advanced Studies
California Lutheran University
Thousand Oaks, CA

About the Authors

Gayle Gregory has been a teacher in elementary, middle, and secondary schools. For many years, she taught in schools with extended periods of instructional time (block schedules). She has had extensive districtwide experience as a curriculum consultant and staff development coordinator. Most recently, she was course director at York University for the Faculty of Education, teaching in the teacher education program. She now consults internationally (Europe, Asia, North and South America, Australia) with teachers, administrators, and staff developers in the areas of brain-compatible learning, block scheduling, emotional intelligence, instructional and assessment practices, cooperative group learning, presentation skills, renewal of secondary schools, enhancing teacher quality, coaching and mentoring, and managing change. She is affiliated with many organizations, including the Association for Supervision and Curriculum Development and the National Staff Development Council, and is the coauthor of *Designing Brain-Compatible Learning* and *Thinking Inside the Block Schedule: Strategies for Teaching in Extended Periods of Time*. She has been featured in Video Journal of Education's edition on *Differentiated Instruction*. She is committed to lifelong learning and professional growth for herself and others. She may be contacted by calling (905) 336-6565 or by e-mail: gregorygayle@netscape.net. Her Web site is www3.sympatico.ca/gayle.gregory

Carolyn Chapman continues her life's goal to teach as an international educational consultant and trainer. She supports educators in their process of change for today's students. She has taught in kindergarten to college classrooms. Her interactive, hands-on professional development opportunities focus on challenging the mind to ensure success for learners of all ages. Carolyn walks her walk and talks her talk to make a difference in the journey of learning in today's classrooms. Carolyn authored *If the Shoe Fits ... How to Develop Multiple Intelligence in the Classroom*. She has coauthored *Multiple Assessments for Multiple Intelligence, Multiple Intelligence through Centers and Projects, Infusing Reading in the Upper Grades, Content Writing in the Upper Grades*, and *Test Success in the Brain Compatible Classroom*. She is featured in Video Journal of Education's edition on *Differentiated Instruction*. Carolyn's company, Creative Learning Connection, Inc., has also produced a CD, *Carolyn Chapman's: Making the Shoe Fit*. Each of these publications demonstrates Carolyn's yearning and determination to make an effective impact for educators and students. She may be contacted by calling (706) 597-0706 or at her web site www.carolynchapman.com.

Introduction:
One Size Doesn't Fit All

No one would ever say that all students are the same. Certainly no teacher or parent would tell you that. Yet in schools we often treat students as if they were, even though all those faces look so different. We sometimes put them through the same hoops, even though we know it isn't making a difference for all of them. Experience as well as the research we now have about the human brain tell us that students are different, that they learn differently and have different likes, preferences, and needs.

We have used the analogy of "one size doesn't fit all" for years in education. We know that students are different one from the other in height, size, shape, hair and eye color, and background and experience. As with clothing we would not buy or make the same garment for all learners (even school uniforms, although they look the same, are sized and adjusted and accessorized for the wearer) because they would not fit, suit,

Figure 0.1. As With Clothing, So With Lessons: One Size Does Not Fit All.

or be comfortable. Students differ from each other in physical abilities and social development as well. Yet for years we have planned "The Lesson" and taught it to all, knowing that we were boring some and losing others because they were not ready for that learning. Still we expect students to adjust to the learning when the learning should really be adjusted to the learner. Adjustments should be based on sound knowledge of the learner. This includes what they know already, can do, like, are like, need, or prefer.

Our quest in schools and classrooms everywhere is to foster success for students in their lives through becoming self-directed, productive problem solvers, and thinkers. For years we have been studying and implementing research based instructional strategies and assessment tools that make a difference in student achievement. Differentiation is a philosophy that enables teachers to plan strategically in order to reach the needs of the diverse learners in classrooms today to achieve targeted standards. Differentiation is not a set of tools but a philosophy that a teacher embraces to reach the unique needs of every learner.

A differentiated classroom is one in which the teacher responds to those needs (Tomlinson, 1999). Differentiated instruction gives a variety of options to successfully reach targeted standards. It meets learners where they are and offers challenging, appropriate options for them in order to achieve success.

Teachers can differentiate:

♦ The content that students learn

♦ The assessment tools being used

♦ The performance tasks selected

♦ The instructional strategies used

As in clothing "one size doesn't fit all," so in classrooms one way is not the way.

WHY DIFFERENTIATION?

We have been faced with more change than ever before in education. Several decades ago, teachers came into the profession with a desire to work with children, a knowledge base and good intentions. Today, teachers face a challenging landscape that is in constant flux. Many factors influence the constantly changing classroom:

♦ Standard-based classrooms: targeted expectations set by districts, states and nations

♦ High expectations for all students: no longer can we leave children behind and just "spray and pray" for success

♦ Multicultural diversity: continuous influx of immigrant children with little or no communication skills or competencies in English

♦ Student diversity: unique learning styles and different levels of multiple intelligence

♦ New cognitive research on human learning: knowledge of the brain and how it processes memory and makes meaning

♦ Rapid societal and technological change: political and economic revolutions that influence what and how learning takes place

Along with all these changes schools are expected to put the "C.A.R.T. before the horse." The acronym C.A.R.T. stands for

C onnected, Competence, Confidence, Compassion
A cceptance, Affection, Appreciation
R eading, 'Riting and 'Rithmetic,
    and also Responsibility, Respect, and Relationships
T hinking, Technology, Teamwork

All these C.A.R.T. skills and attributes are necessary to be successful in life, not just at school. Schools are expected to build in opportunities within the curriculum to practice and develop these skills. However, the balancing act is dealing with district and state standards and the reality that classrooms contain a diverse, heterogeneous group of learners. Learners who have different cultural backgrounds, different experiences, interests, learning styles, and multiple intelligences are the norm.

They don't all learn the "same thing in the same way on the same day." As educators in classrooms we need to consider each child within the learning community based on his/her needs based on readiness, preferences, and interests.

In this book we explore the elements needed in the classroom to engage students and facilitate learning to increase the chances that all learners will succeed.

Figure 0.2 organizes these elements in categories listing tools and strategies that build an inclusive, nurturing classroom and allows teachers to design learning to honor the diversity of the learning population.

Figure 0.2. Tools and Strategies for Designing Inclusive Classrooms for Diverse Learners

Climate	Knowing the Learner	Assessing the Learner	Adjustable Assignments	Instructional Strategies	Curriculum Approaches
• Safe • Nurturing • Encourages risk taking • Inclusive • Multi-sensory • Stimulating • Complex • Challenging • Collaborative • Questioning • Cubing **Team and Class Building** **Norms**	• **Learning styles** Dunn & Dunn Gregorc 4Mat Silver/Strong/ Hanson • **Multiple Intelligences** Using observation checklists, inventories, logs and journals to become more aware of how one learns	• **Before:** **Formal** Written pre-test Journaling Surveys/Inventories **Informal** Squaring off Boxing Graffiti Facts • **During:** **Formal** Journaling/Portfolios Teacher-made tests Checklists/Rubrics **Informal** Thumb it Fist of five Face the fact • **After:** **Formal** Post test Portfolio/Conferences Reflections **Informal** Talking Topics Conversation Circles Donut	Compacting **T. A. P. S.** **Total Group:** Lecturette Presentation Demonstration Jigsaw Video Field Trip Guest Speaker Text **Alone:** • Interest • Personalized • Multiple intelligences **Paired:** • Random • Interest • Task **Small Groups:** • Heterogeneous • Homogeneous • Task Oriented • Constructed • Random • Interest	• **Brain/Research Based** Memory model Elaborative rehearsal • Focus activities • Graphic organizers Compare & contrast Webbing • Metaphors • Cooperative group learning • Jigsaw • Role Play	Centers Projects **Problem Based** Inquiry Contracts

PLANNING FOR DIFFERENTIATED INSTRUCTION

A planning model (Figure 0.3) can be used to help teachers make decisions about differentiated instruction and assessment. Each phase of the planning model will be explained and throughout this book the strategies are clarified using examples.

1. Of course the first thing that is considered in planning is the standards, outcomes, or expectations. It should be clear what the students should know, be able to do, or be like after the learning experience. Assessment strategies are identified so that data may be collected ongoing (logs, checklists, journals, observations, portfolios, rubrics).

Essential questions may be developed that will be visible and posted throughout the unit so that students can consider the question as they work on tasks.

2. Content will be identified including facts and vocabulary as well as essential skills.

3. Activate—Teachers will design opportunities to activate prior knowledge and pre-assess so that the teacher is more knowledgeable to begin planning the learning. This may be done 2 or 3 weeks prior to the unit to allow plenty of time for planning learning activities, grouping students, and raising anticipation about the new topic. "Emotional hooks" can be used to engage and to capture attention of the students through challenge, novelty and unique experiences.

4. Acquire—Decisions need to be made about what new information and skills students need to learn and how they will acquire the knowledge. Teachers also decide whether the acquisition will be in a total group setting or in small groups.

5. Apply and Adjust—Students need the opportunity to practice and become actively engaged with the new learning in order to understand and retain it. The teacher will decide on how the students will be grouped and what tasks they will be assigned to challenge them at the appropriate level.

6. Assess—The teacher will decide (or provide choices) as to how the students will demonstrate knowledge or competencies.

All of these decisions are made with the intention of honoring the diversity of the learners be it learning styles, multiple intelligences, or personal interests.

So let's get started exploring the facets of differentiating instruction and offering our students diverse opportunities to succeed.

Figure 0.3. The Six-Step Planning Model for Differentiated Learning

PLANNING FOR DIFFERENTIATED LEARNING

1. STANDARDS: What should students know and be able to do?	Assessment tools for data collection: (logs, checklists, journals, agendas, observations, portfolios, rubrics, contracts)

Essential Questions:

2. CONTENT: (concepts, vocabulary, facts)	**SKILLS:**

3. ACTIVATE: Focus Activity: Preassessment Prior knowledge & engaging the learners	Pre-assessment strategy	• Quiz, test • Surveys • K.W.L. • Journals • Arm Gauge • Give me 5 • Brainstorm • Concept Formation • Thumb it
4. ACQUIRE: Total group or small groups		• Lecturette • Presentation • Demonstration • Jigsaw • Video • Field Trip • Guest Speaker • Text

Grouping Decisions: (T.A.P.S. random, heterogeneous, homogeneous, interest, task, constructed)

5. APPLY ADJUST			• Learning Centers • Projects • Contracts • Compact/Enrichment • Problem Based • Inquiry • Research • Independent study
6. ASSESS			• Quiz, test, • Performance • Products • Presentation • Demonstration • Log, journal • Checklist • Portfolio • Rubric • Metacognition

Diversity Honored (Learning Styles, Multiple Intelligences, personal interest, etc.)

Creating a Climate for Learning 1

Classrooms everywhere offer a diversity of faces and shapes and sizes, but underneath the diversity there are fundamental elements that all learners need in order to succeed and to feel positive about their experiences in school.

WHAT DO LEARNERS NEED TO SUCCEED?

For students to succeed, they need to believe that they can learn, and that what they are learning is useful, relevant, and meaningful for them. They need to know that they belong in the classroom and that they are responsible for their own learning as well as their own behavior. In *Education on the Edge of Possibility*, the Caines (Caine & Caine, 1997) state,

> Teachers' beliefs in and about human potential and in the ability of all children to learn and achieve are critical. These aspects of the teachers' mental models have a profound impact on the learning climate and learner states of mind that teachers create. Teachers need to understand students' feelings and attitudes will be involved and will profoundly influence student learning. (p. 124)

Effective teachers believe that all students can learn and can be successful. Effective teachers consciously create a climate where all students feel included. Effective teachers believe that there is potential in each learner and commit to finding the key that will unlock that potential.

CLASSROOM CULTURE AND LEARNING COMMUNITIES

Culture is often referred to as "the way we do things around here." People who live and work in a culture sometimes can't explain or describe it, but they can certainly sense it. Culture may not necessarily be conveyed only through words but also through actions. Sometimes what we do screams so loudly that we can't hear what is being said. In the words of DePorter, Reardon, and Singer-Nourie (1998) in their book *Quantum Teaching, "Everything Speaks, Everything Always."* They caution teachers that what they do, say, and allude to have an effect on learners and their perception of success. According to Parry and Gregory (1998),

> As far as the brain is concerned, actions speak louder than words. Everything that happens in the classroom is monitored by three parts of the brain, two of which have no spoken language but are very adept at reading body language and tone of voice. Every gesture, every inflection, and every invasion of personal space is monitored by the limbic system and evaluated in terms of its threat potential. These skills allowed our ancestors to survive and they are still alive and well in all of us. (p. 13)

Because our brain is a parallel processor, it absorbs information on a conscious and an unconscious level. The brain constantly performs many functions at the same time (Ornstein & Thompson, 1984). It therefore can manage to process thoughts, emotions, and perceptions simultaneously.

The brain is also a parallel processor in that it facilitates learning by involving both focused attention and peripheral perception. O'Keefe and Nadel (1978) state that the brain responds to the entire sensory context in which learning takes place. A peripheral stimulus includes everything in the classroom from the drab or colorful walls to subtle clues such as a look or gesture that conveys meaning and is interpreted by the brain. All sounds and visual signals are full of complex messages. A sarcastic remark or gesture can speak volumes to a sensitive learner. It conveys far more than the spoken word.

In his work with the Midcontinent Research for Education and Learning (McREL) group and with Dimensions of Learning, Robert Marzano examined the climate for learning, as did Jay McTighe:

Closely related to teachers' behavior is the development of a classroom climate conducive to good thinking . . . students cannot think well in a harsh, threatening situation or even in a subtly intimidating environment where group pressure makes independent thinking unlikely. Teachers can make their classrooms more thoughtful places by demonstrating in their actions that they welcome originality and differences of opinion.

Noted researcher Deborah Rozman remarked in 1998 that "the neural information the heart sends to the brain can either facilitate or inhibit cortical function, affecting perception, emotional response, learning and decision making." The heartbeat of another person is perceivable within three to four feet because of the electromagnetic field that it projects. The heartbeat of one person registers in the brain waves of another person. There are intuitive or gut feelings that are picked up by neurons throughout the body. "People need to know you care before they care what you know" has often been said. And old adages become just that because they are usually true.

In *Choice Theory of Motivation*, William Glasser (1990) cites five equally important needs:

♦ The need to survive and reproduce

♦ The need to belong and love

♦ The need to have some power

♦ The need to have freedom

♦ The need to have fun

This is also evident in Abraham Maslow's well-known hierarchy of needs (Maslow, 1968), which includes the following in a hierarchy beginning with the most basic:

♦ Physiological needs: food, water, air, shelter

♦ Safety needs: security, freedom from fear, order

♦ Belongingness and love: friends, spouse, children

♦ Self-esteem: self-respect, achievement, reputation

♦ Self-actualization: to become what the individual has the potential to become

Human beings generally move up the hierarchy from basic to complex needs. As each need has been met, it becomes less of a motivator as the person focuses on the next level.

As we examine motivators we need to remember that basic needs have to be met first for students. We recognize that all humans have a very strong need to be liked and included. Classrooms everywhere must foster an inclusionary climate. It is essential that students bond with one another and with the teacher to form a positive learning community. Dr. Robert Sapolsky (1998), Professor of Biological Sciences and Neuroscience at Stanford University, states that we can minimize the impact of stress by building a supportive environment:

> Put an infant primate through something unpleasant: it gets a stress-response. Put it through the same stressor while in a room full of other primates and . . . it depends. If those primates are strangers, the stress-response gets worse. But if they are friends, the stress-response is decreased. Social support networks—it helps to have a shoulder to cry on, a hand to hold, an ear to listen to you, someone to cradle you and to tell you it will be okay. (p. 215)

Some teachers, with their students, cooperatively develop classroom "agreements" (Gibbs, 1995), or "Trust Statements" (Harmin, 1994), or "rules to live by" to help students feel that they have a voice in the running of the classroom. These rules also help students become more emotionally intelligent and responsible learners. Students in small groups generate statements that they believe the class should live by—for example, "Everyone's ideas count." After the groups share their statements, the class combines, deletes, or adds sentences until consensus is reached and students feel comfortable and can support these rules to live by, which may include the following:

- ◆ There is no wrong opinion.
- ◆ No put-downs or sarcasm here.
- ◆ Everyone must be heard.
- ◆ Mistakes are learning points.

If these statements are posted for all students to see and reflect on, students will monitor and honor the rules that they have created.

We also recognize that learning communities foster links between heart and mind. Driscoll (1994) asks us to consider that "community is the entity in which individuals derive meaning. It is not so much characterized by shared space as it is by shared meanings. Community in this view is not a mere artifact of people living (or working or studying) in the same place, but is rather a rich source of 'living tradition'" (p. 3).

EMOTIONS AND LEARNING

Students living in fear cannot learn. We know from the research on the phenomenon of "downshifting the psychophysiological response to threat associated with fatigue or perceived helplessness" (Caine & Caine, 1997, p. 18) that students will not attend to learning if their major concern is safety.

Safety in classrooms means intellectual safety as well as physical safety. During stress, the emotional centers of the brain take control of cognitive functioning and thus the rational thinking part of the brain is not as efficient, and this can cause learning to be impeded. If students are living daily with the threat of being ridiculed or bullied, they cannot give their full attention to learning. Students who are challenged beyond their skill level are more concerned about being embarrassed or laughed at than with the quest for learning. They will not be motivated to attempt the challenge if they aren't able to imagine or perceive success.

In classrooms where the teacher does not adjust the learning to the level of readiness and teaches only to the "middle," some students will be bored from lack of challenge and others may "downshift" from too great a challenge. Thus teachers need to consider where their learners are in relation to the learning goal and to plan learning experiences just beyond the skill level of each student.

All students are more likely to be engaged in the learning, rise to the challenge, and have a sense of self-confidence as they approach the task if they feel that they have a chance to succeed. Thus once the levels of readiness have been considered (although it is unrealistic to consider each learner individually), students can often be grouped and experiences designed to accommodate the learners at their level of understanding.

Teachers need to consider the degree of complexity of learning tasks so that they will be challenging but not overwhelming. This establishes the state of "flow" (Csikszentmihalyi, 1990), the condition that exists when learners are so engaged, excited about learning, challenged, and receiving appropriate feedback that they are oblivious to anything else. Students are at their most productive and most creative in this state:

> People seem to concentrate best when the demands on them are a bit greater than usual, and they are able to give more than usual. If there is too little demand on them, people are bored. If there is too much for them to handle, they get anxious. Flow occurs in that delicate zone between boredom and anxiety. (Goleman, 1992, cited in Csikszentmihalyi, 1990, p. 4)

Renata Caine, a well-known pioneer in the field of brain-based education, proposes that there are three basic elements to brain/mind learning and teaching:

♦ Emotional climate and relationship or relaxed alertness

♦ Instruction or immersion in complex experience

♦ Consolidation of learning or active processing

Emotional climate and relationships are important to produce what Kohn (1993) refers to as "relaxed alertness":

> All the methodologies that are used to orchestrate the learning context influence the state of relaxed alertness. It is particularly important for educators to understand the effect of rewards and punishments on student states of mind. Research shows most applications of reward and punishment in the behavioral mode inhibit creativity, interfere with intrinsic motivation, and reduce the likelihood of meaningful learning. (cited in Caine & Caine, 1997, p. 123)

Rewards and punishments tend to lessen the chances of self-motivation and an appreciation of learning is its own reward. Five practical alternatives to using rewards are the following:

♦ Eliminating threat

♦ Creating a strongly positive climate

♦ Increasing feedback

♦ Setting goals

♦ Activating and engaging positive emotions (Jensen, 1998b, p. 68)

It is important, if not imperative, that students feel good, have success, have friends, and celebrate their learning:

> Emotions affect student behavior because they create distinct, mind-body states. A state is a moment composed of a specific posture, breathing rate, and chemical balance in the body. The presence or absence of norepinephrine, vasopressin, testosterone, serotonin, progesterone, dopamine, and dozens of other chemicals dramatically alters your frame of mind and body. How important are states to us? They are all that we have; they are our feelings, desires, memories, and motivations. (Jensen, 1998b, p. 75)

The emotional environment interacts with instruction and influences how information is consolidated. If "downshifting" occurs, the high stress/threat response sabotages connections and thus learning cannot take place. At this point we are fortunate if even memorization of isolated facts and programmed skills is possible. It is almost impossible for higher-order thinking to take place.

If students think that success isn't possible because the task is too difficult or instructions for a task are ambiguous and not understood, they feel uncertain. These situations cause the learner to form a negative state, and the learner ceases to persevere. Alternately, classrooms that create "eustress" or a state of "flow" create a positive learning environment. Classrooms that embed choices in learning and routines that demonstrate mutual respect are supportive learning environments for students.

EMOTIONAL INTELLIGENCE

Emotional intelligence is a person's ability to use his or her emotions intelligently. It involves maintaining a balance between reason and emotion. Daniel Goleman (1990) organizes emotional intelligence as a set of emotional competencies that occur in five domains:

Self-Awareness

Self-awareness is one's ability to sense and name a feeling when it happens and also to put it into words. Self-aware people can use appropriate strategies to deal with their moods by sharing frustrations with others or seeking support on a bad day. Teachers should encourage students to articulate their feelings and seek and give support. Self-awareness is also being in touch with feelings, not letting feelings become engulfing, and having strategies to cope with moods. In her book *Molecules of Emotion*, Candace B. Pert (1998) suggests, "Feeling low and sluggish? Take a walk. Feeling anxious and jittery? Run!" (p. 293) We all need to find ways to change and manage our moods once we recognize what they are.

Managing Emotions

Managing emotions is an outcome of recognizing and labeling feelings. It is the ability to calm and soothe during anxious moments or to manage and deal with anger. Using "teachable moments" (when an inappropriate emotional response has been given), teachers can help students learn problem-solving skills to generate appropriate alternatives to the feelings. Conflict resolution is easier if students have a repertoire of strategies for dealing with conflict when it erupts.

Self-Motivation

Self-motivation consists of competencies such as persistence, setting one's own goals, and delaying gratification. Many students give up very easily when difficulties occur. Students need to feel hopeful even in the face of setback. The state of "flow" is an integral component of this domain. If students and teachers can create that state of high challenge and low threat, more learning can take place.

Empathy

Empathy is being able to feel for another. Teachers can ask students to "stand in the other person's shoes." These people may be classmates in a situation that calls for empathy. They may be characters in fiction or history with whom students can empathize to understand their emotions. This allows the students to feel how the character or individual might have felt. Understanding another's point of view or perspective is often a standard targeted in many districts. Feeling for others builds tolerance and understanding.

Social Skills

Social skills are the competencies that one uses to "read" other people and manage emotional interactions. People with high levels of social competencies have the ability to handle relationships well and are able to adapt to a variety of social situations. They are said to have "social polish." Teachers modeling these competencies and labeling them when seen in the classroom show the value of emotional intelligence in personal interactions.

INSTRUCTIONAL TECHNIQUE: QUESTIONING

Downshifting can occur during teacher-student question and answer sessions. Fear of ridicule occurs when students are challenged by questions that are beyond their level of understanding or comprehension. The notion of "wait time" (Rowe, 1988) gives students time to access information stored in long-term memory. We know this takes at least 3 to 5 seconds. The quality or quantity of the answer is often increased by the amount of time given in order to access the information and formulate an answer. Generally the longer the "think time," the better the answer.

"Think, Pair, Share" (Lyman & McTighe, 1988)is an obvious technique to use to facilitate wait time. Asking students to think by themselves, pair with another student, and share their ideas naturally gives students time to think, access information, and formulate better answers. This also decreases the chances of downshifting and increases the chances of the students actually thinking about and attending to the question that has been posed. It encourages all students to share thinking, not just the person called on to answer. As the teacher comes to know the learners better and to recognize their levels of readiness, questions can be differentiated by level of complexity. This challenges learners at or just beyond their levels of comprehension or experience.

Often, teachers ask questions or pose problems at different levels of Bloom's thinking taxonomy (Bloom et al., 1956), for example,

♦ Level I, Knowledge-Recall: What is the story about?

♦ Level II, Comprehension-Understanding: Why did this happen?

♦ Level III, Application-Transfer: Use the information to predict . . .

♦ Level IV, Analysis-Examining: How many elements are present?

♦ Level V, Synthesis-Combining: Change the story to a new setting.

♦ Level VI, Evaluation-Rating: Rank all the solutions in priority order.

Figure 1.1 suggests stems that may be used at each level of Bloom's taxonomy. Teachers may differentiate questions based on students' readiness and level of comprehension. The figure also provides suggestions for tasks at different levels of the taxonomy.

INSTRUCTIONAL TECHNIQUE: CUBING

Cubing is another technique that can help students think at different levels of the taxonomy (Cowan & Cowan, 1980). Cubing is a technique for considering a subject from six points of view (Cowan & Cowan, 1980; Tomlinson, 2001). Cubing works well when we are "stuck" or locked into a particular way of thinking.

One side of the cube may say: Describe it
Another side: Compare it
The third side: Associate it
The fourth side: Analyze it
The fifth side: Apply it
And the sixth side says: Argue for or against it

Cubes may vary with tasks or commands that are appropriate to the level of readiness of the group. Cubes may also be constructed with tasks in a particular area of the multiple intelligences such as verbal/linguistic, bodily/kinesthetic, or intrapersonal intelligence.

Figure 1.1. Question Starters and Classroom Activities Differentiated According to Bloom's Taxonomy

QUESTION STARTERS

Level I: KNOWLEDGE (Recall)

1. What is the definition for . . . ?
2. What happened after . . . ?
3. Recall the facts.
4. What were the characteristics of . . . ?
5. Which is true or false?
6. How many . . . ?
7. Who was the . . . ?
8. Tell in your own words.

Level II: COMPREHENSION

1. Why are these ideas similar?
2. In your own words retell the story of . . .
3. What do you think could happen?
4. How are these ideas different?
5. Explain what happened after.
6. What are some examples?
7. Can you provide a definition of . . . ?
8. Who was the key character?

Level III: APPLICATION (applying without understanding is not effective)

1. What is another instance of . . . ?
2. Demonstrate the way to . . .
3. Which one is most like . . . ?
4. What questions would you ask?
5. Which factors would you change?
6. Could this have happened in . . . ? Why or why not?
7. How would you organize these ideas?

POTENTIAL ACTIVITIES

1. Describe the . . .
2. Make a time line of events
3. Make a facts chart
4. Write a list of . . . steps in . . . facts about . . .
5. List all the people in the story.
6. Make a chart showing . . .
7. Make an acrostic
8. Recite a poem.

1. Cut out or draw pictures to show an event.
2. Illustrate what you think the main idea was.
3. Make a cartoon strip showing the sequence of . . .
4. Write and perform a play based on the . . .
5. Compare this _____ with _____
6. Construct a model of . . .
7. Write a news report.
8. Prepare a flow chart to show the sequence . . .

1. Construct a model to demonstrate using it.
2. Make a display to illustrate one event.
3. Make a collection about . . .
4. Design a relief map to include relevant information about an event.
5. Scan a collection of photographs to illustrate a particular aspect of the study.
6. Create a mural to depict . . .

QUESTION STARTERS

Level IV: ANALYSIS

1. What are the component parts of . . . ?
2. What steps are important in the process of . . . ?
3. If . . . then . . .
4. What other conclusions can you reach about . . . that have not been mentioned?
5. The difference between the fact and the hypothesis is . . .
6. The solution would be to . . .
7. What is the relationship between . . . and . . . ?

Level V: SYNTHESIS

1. Can you design a . . . ?
2. Why not compose a song about . . . ?
3. Why don't you devise your own way to . . . ?
4. Can you create new and unusual uses for . . . ?
5. Can you develop a proposal for . . . ?
6. How would you deal with . . . ?
7. Invent a scheme that would . . .

Level VI: EVALUATION

1. In your opinion . . .
2. Appraise the chances for . . .
3. Grade or rank the . . .
4. What do you think should be the outcome?
5. What solution do you favor and why?
6. Which systems are best? Worst?
7. Rate the relative value of these ideas to . . .
8. Which is the better bargain?

POTENTIAL ACTIVITIES

1. Design a questionnaire about . . .
2. Conduct an investigation to produce . . .
3. Make a flow chart to show . . .
4. Construct a graph to show . . .
5. Put on a play about . . .
6. Review . . . in terms of identified criteria.
7. Prepare a report about the area of study.

1. Create a model that shows your new ideas.
2. Devise an original plan or experiment for . . .
3. Finish the incomplete . . .
4. Make a hypothesis about . . .
5. Change . . . so that it will . . .
6. Propose a method to . . .
7. Prescribe a way to . . .
8. Give the book a new title.

1. Prepare a list of criteria you would use to judge a . . . Indicate priority ratings you would give.
2. Conduct a debate about an issue.
3. Prepare an annotated bibliography . . .
4. Form a discussion panel on the topic of . . .
5. Prepare a case to present your opinions about . . .
6. List some common assumptions about . . . Rationalize your reactions.

Why Do We Use Cubes?

Cubing, with its many sides, allows students to look at an issue or topic from a variety of angles and to develop a multidimensional perspective rather than a single one.

Cubes offer a chance to differentiate learning by readiness (familiarity with content or level of skill), student interest, and/or learning profile (multiple intelligences). Cubes may vary in color and tasks depending on the abilities and interest of the small group. They add an element of novelty and fun to the learning by providing uniqueness to the lesson. It is a great strategy for tactile/kinesthetic learners as they reinforce understanding and extend or demonstrate learning.

How Do We Use Cubes?

1. Keep clear learning goals in mind when considering the use of cubing for different learners.

2. Provide extended opportunities, materials, and learning situations that are appropriate for a wide range of readiness, interests, and learning styles.

3. Make sure students understand the verbs and directions for the tasks.

4. Group students according to readiness, with different colored cubes giving tasks or questions appropriate to their level of understanding and ability level in that particular topic or skill. Students assist one another in their learning.

5. Ask students to share findings with the large group or to form base groups of experts to share their tasks.

Figure 1.2 suggests verbs that may be used on all six sides of a cube.

Cubing may also be differentiated using multiple intelligences. Cubes may be designed with a variety of multiple intelligence activities to give students a chance to use their varied strengths. As an alternative, teachers can also use a die with numbers 1 to 6 and provide students with activity cards at various levels of complexity related to the topic (Figure 1.3).

If students are studying the planets, for example, they might have a variety of cubes in the different multiple intelligences to process information for musical rhythmic intelligence, bodily kinesthetic intelligence, visual spatial intelligence, naturalist, logical mathematical, interpersonal, or intrapersonal intelligences. Or in a class where students are reading *Charlotte's Web* by E. B. White, cubes could be used to deal with visual spa-

Figure 1.2. Use Of Different Verbs, Tasks, and Commands on Each Side of a Cube

Cubing . . . Levels of Thinking	
1. Tell 　**Describe** 　**Recall** 　**Name** 　**Locate** 　**List**	**4. Review** 　**Discuss** 　**Prepare** 　**Diagram** 　**Cartoon**
2. Compare 　**Contrast** 　**Example** 　**Explain** 　**Define** 　**Write**	**5. Propose** 　**Suggest** 　**Finish** 　**Prescribe** 　**Devise**
3. Connect 　**Make** 　**Design** 　**Produce** 　**Develop**	**6. Debate** 　**Formulate** 　**Choose** 　**Support** 　**In your opinion . . .**

tial intelligence, and students could be given the following statements on the sides of their cubes:

Green Cube

1. Draw Charlotte as you think she looks.

2. Use a Venn diagram and compare Charlotte and Fern.

3. Use a comic strip to tell what happened in this chapter.

4. Shut your eyes and describe the barn. Jot down your ideas.

5. Predict what will happen in the next chapter. Use symbols.

6. In your opinion, why is Charlotte a good friend?

Figure 1.3.   Cubes Vary in Color and Tasks Depending on the Abilities
and Interests of the Learners

Green Cube	Blue Cube
1.	1.
2.	2.
3.	3.
4.	4.
5.	5.
6.	6.
Yellow Cube	**Red Cube**
1.	1.
2.	2.
3.	3.
4.	4.
5.	5.
6.	6.

Yellow Cube

1. Use a graphics program on the computer and create a character web for Wilbur.

2. Use symbols on a Venn diagram to compare Wilbur and Charlotte.

3. Use a storyboard to show the progress of the plot to this point.

4. Draw the farm and label the items, people, and buildings.

5. What is the message that you think the writer wants people to remember? Draw a symbol that illustrates your idea.

6. When you think of the title, do you agree or disagree that it is a good choice? Why or why not?

Both cubes are tapping into using visual spatial intelligence, with the green cube working at a more basic level with key aspects of the story and the yellow cube stretching student thinking more in the abstraction, extending ideas and making connections.

CLASSROOM CLIMATE

Physical and Emotional Atmosphere

The climate is influenced by the physical attributes of the classroom.

Things such as appropriate lighting, cleanliness, orderliness, and displays of students' work contribute to that positive atmosphere. Plentiful and appropriate resources are necessary to facilitate student success. There could be computers and materials that allow for hands-on manipulation. There should be opportunities for social interaction and intellectual growth.

Enriched environments are created not only by materials but also by the complexity and variety of tasks and challenges and feedback (Caine & Caine, 1997; Jensen, 1998b). Engaging materials and activities help to develop dendritic growth, the neural connections that are facilitated by experiences and stimulation (Diamond & Hopson, 1998; Green, Greenough, & Schlumpf, 1983; Healy, 1992). Dr. Arnold B. Scheibel, Professor of Neurology at UCLA, suggests that

on the basis of what we know and have seen from animal experiments, it seems a likely inference that the same phenomenon in rats, mice, cats, and monkeys holds for humans, as well: Increase the level of environmental stimulation and challenge, and you will increase the branching of the dendrites and the thickness of the human cortex. (Diamond & Hopson, 1998, p. 35)

This growth is stimulated by a variety of complex and intriguing activities, as previously noted by Renata Caine. "If we encourage children to make choices from a selected variety of available challenges, both environmental and intellectual, we are no doubt following the wisest course" (Healy, 1992, p. 72).

Use of Music

Another component for enhancing classroom climate may be the inclusion of music. Researchers at Strathclyde University have discovered that brainpower soars when students listen to stimulating pop tunes and advise that playing the latest hits in classrooms may actually increase student achievement.

This study by Dr. Brian Boyd and Katrina Bowes (Dana: The Brain in the News, 2001) researched the effects of music after learning about studies in Russia that discovered that medical patients who listened to music recovered faster. In contrast to the belief that that only classical music calms the learner, they found that modern music with the same tempo as classical (60 beats per minute) has the same effect and makes the mind more receptive to learning. This music can actually help the brain retain information.

Many teachers who have tried using pop music report higher levels of concentration by their students. Pop music triggers the autonomic nervous system, and we respond by feeling good and tapping our feet to the music. The pupils of the eyes dilate, and endorphin levels and energy rise. Teachers often say that students will learn more in a class if they are enjoying the experience, and music can set the stage for learning. Students will link a known routine with a piece of music and thus be ready for what is to follow. The music can be playful, for example playing Marvin Gaye's "I Heard It Through the Grapevine" while students are estimating the number of raisins in a small lunch-size box. Or the music can appeal to the emotions and create a mood such as happens when listening to "When Johnny Comes Marching Home Again" at the beginning of a discussion of World War I or "War" by Bruce Springsteen in relation to the study of the Vietnam War.

Music energizes people and masks "dead air" when there is a "dip" in the energy level of students. Mozart's music or other Baroque music can soothe and calm as well (Campbell, 1998).

Laughter

Laughter is another tool to use in classrooms. It punctuates learning by releasing neurochemical transmitters called endorphins, and it is said to be the shortest distance between two people. Laughter even helps the immune system to increase the number of type T leukocytes (T cells) in the blood. T cells combat damage and infection, and some researchers have even dubbed them "happiness cells" (Silvia H. Cardoso, Ph.D., in Dana publication *Cerebrum*, 2000). It makes sense to include humor and laughter and to celebrate learning in the classroom. Teachers can encourage students to applaud one another and cheer for each other's successes. Using energizing cheers (Burke, 1994; DePorter, 1998), students give rounds of applause, high fives, and other cheers that students can often create for themselves. These cheers also include actions to supplement the aural responses. Kinesthetic actions help energize by sending more oxygen and glucose to the brain and often result in fun and laughter to raise endorphins.

Even though each learner in the classroom may appear very different on the surface, each needs to feel safe and comfortable. So in classrooms climate and atmosphere play an important part in the learning process. Anything teachers can do to create a risk-free supportive environment where students can feel safe and where they can thrive needs to be considered and implemented in classrooms. Building a community of learners who care for and support one another is essential in a differentiated classroom. Students who know and respect each other are more tolerant of differences and more comfortable when tasks are different. Even though "one size doesn't fit all," learners require all these conditions to succeed.

Knowing 2
the Learner

We look in classrooms at schools and observe the variety of students in all different shapes and sizes. They all look different, and they are. As with clothing, their sizes vary and each wearer has individual preferences for style, color, and occasion.

Could we buy clothing for children we didn't know? We would need to find out about them as individuals, ask about their likes and dislikes, preferences for color and style, and of course their sizes. We would never consider buying just anything and hope that it would fit and appeal to the recipient. So in classrooms, we need to know the learners so that we can make sure the curriculum fits.

Many teachers have spent summers writing and designing curriculum that focuses on standards and is intended to engage learners. But when they met the students in the classroom, the program didn't fit their needs or appeal to them (or, it might be said, "They sent the wrong students"). It is important to look at the reality in our classrooms, recognizing that each learner is unique and that what would engage or intrigue one learner wouldn't have the slightest chance of capturing the attention of another student. Part of the reason for this situation is that students have "designer brains," as noted cognitive researcher Robert Sylwester (1995) points out. That is to say, their brains differ as much as their fingerprints and faces do. Over the years a variety of experts have shared with educators the notion of student learning styles and the fact that we all learn in different ways, process information differently, and have distinct preferences about where, when, and how we learn.

LEARNING STYLES

To examine how students access, process, and express information most easily, we look at theories of learning styles and multiple intelligences. As more information about each student's learning styles, modalities, multiple intelligences, and thinking styles is gathered, it allows teachers to use the knowledge of student strengths as an entry point for instruction and to capture attention.

It is also important for students to increase their knowledge of themselves and for teachers to help students develop metacognitive skills for self-assessment and learning for life. Knowing how one learns is necessary information if one is to learn throughout life. Research on instructional strategies at the Maryland State Department of Education indicates that "teachers who help students develop and internalize metacognitve strategies through direct instruction, modeling, and practice promote learning because the effective use of such strategies is one of the primary differences between more and less able learners" (McTighe, 1990).

One learning-styles model developed by Rita Dunn and Ken Dunn (1987) classifies learning styles as auditory, visual, tactile, and kinesthetic:

♦ **Auditory Learners.** Auditory learners absorb spoken and heard material easily and like to be involved in aural questioning rather than reading materials. They prefer listening to lectures, stories, and songs, and they enjoy variation such as voice inflection and intonational pitch. They like to discuss and use opportunities to talk about their learning with other students.

♦ **Visual Learners.** Visual learners learn best from information that they see or read. They like illustrations, pictures, and diagrams. Graphic organizers are useful tools for them to construct meaning visually. Color has an impact on their learning.

♦ **Tactile Learners.** Tactile learners learn best from handling materials, writing, drawing, and being involved with concrete experiences.

♦ **Kinesthetic Learners.** Kinesthetic learners learn best by doing and moving, by becoming physically involved in learning activities that are meaningful and relevant in their lives.

♦ **Tactile/Kinesthetic Learners**. Tactile/kinesthetic learners want to be physically involved in the learning process. They enjoy role-playing and simulations and like the freedom and opportunity to move about the classroom.

The more teachers can involve all modalities and learning styles, the more chances we have of engaging learners in using their whole brains.

Figure 2.1. Learning Styles: Learning Is Affected by Such Factors as Time of Day and Environment

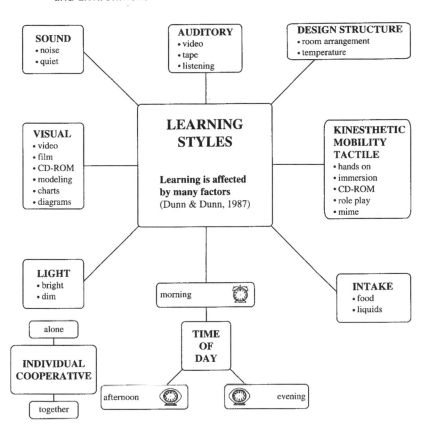

Teachers also need to consider other factors that affect learning styles:

♦ Noise level: Do students prefer noise or quiet?

♦ Design structure: What is the preferred room arrangement? Is the room too hot or cold?

♦ Motivation and persistence: Are they able to engage for long or short periods of time?

♦ Responsibility: Are they fairly independent and self-directed, or do they need a lot of guidance?

♦ Structure: Do they prefer to have more flexibility, or do they need detailed structure?

♦ Individual/Peer: Do they like to work with others, or do they prefer to learn alone?

Teachers also can use a learning inventory (see Figure 2.2) to get more data about learners and their needs. Just the knowledge that there are preferences should influence teachers' plans for presenting a variety of material and designing practice in the classroom with options and choices.

THINKING STYLES

Anthony Gregorc (1982) at the University of Connecticut has developed a theory of thinking styles based on two variables: the way we view the world (whether we see the world in an abstract or concrete way) and the way we order the world (in a sequential or random order). Using these variables, Gregorc combines them to create four styles of thinking:

♦ **Concrete Random Thinkers.** These thinkers, who enjoy experimentation, are also known as divergent thinkers. They are eager to take intuitive leaps in order to create. They have a need to find alternate ways of doing things. Thus in the classroom these types of thinkers need to be allowed to have opportunities to make choices about their learning and about how they demonstrate understandings. These learners enjoy creating new models and practical things that result from their new learning and concept development.

♦ **Concrete Sequential Thinkers.** These thinkers are based in the physical world identified through their senses. They are detail oriented, notice details, and recall them with ease. They require structure, frameworks, timelines, and organization to their learning. They like lecture and teacher-directed activities.

♦ **Abstract Sequential Thinkers.** These thinkers delight in the world of theory and abstract thought. Their thinking processes are rational, logical, and intellectual. They are happiest when involved with their own work and investigation. These learners need to have the time to examine fully the new ideas, concepts, and theories with which they have been presented. They like to support the new information by investigating and analyzing so that the learning makes sense and has real meaning for them.

♦ **Abstract Random Thinkers.** These thinkers organize information through self-reflection and prefer working in people-oriented, fluid situations. They live in a world of feelings and emotion and learn best when they can personalize information. These learners like to discuss and interact with others as they learn. Cooperative group learning, centers or stations, and partner work facilitate their understanding.

Figure 2.2. How Do You Like to Learn?

1. Do you like music on while you study, or do you prefer a quiet place?
   Quiet   Music

2. Where would you prefer to work on an assignment?
   Classroom   Desk (home)
   On the floor   At a table
   On a computer

3. If you are not able to complete something, is it because
   You forgot?   It's boring?
   You got distracted?   You need help?

4. Where do you like to sit in class?
   Near the door   Front
   By the wall   Near a window
   Back

5. Do you like to work with a partner?
   Why or why not?

6. Are you more alert in the afternoon?
   In the evening?
   In the morning?

7. What classes do you enjoy most and why?

   _____

   _____

   _____

8. Describe how you study. Where? When? How?

   _____

   _____

   _____

9. If you have an assignment due in two weeks, how do you plan to complete it?

   _____

   _____

   _____

10. If something is new for you, do you
    Like to have it explained?   Like to read about it?
    Like to watch a video/   Like to just try it?
    demonstration?

David Kolb (1984) also developed a learning style profile based on Experiential Learning, which includes the following four groups:

1. **Accommodators** like to try out new things and "shake up" their own and others' "boxes." They like to be creative, they are flexible risk takers, and they want to do things "their way."

2. **Convergers** value and want to know only what is useful and relevant to the immediate situation or question. They are good at pulling out and organizing essential information. They like clear goals and specific timelines.

3. **Assimilators** want to investigate, read, research, and learn as much as possible about a topic. They have the patience and tenacity to delve deeply into information, and they enjoy abstract content. They believe that they learn from past experiences and from experts.

4. **Divergers** value positive, caring environments where their surroundings are comfortable. They like to learn from others through conversation and dialogue. They want to explore and seek alternatives, and they are altruistic in their pursuit of learning.

Bernice McCarthy's 4Mat Model (McCarthy, 1990) identifies four learning styles and the type of teaching strategies best suited to each of them: (I) the imaginative learner, (II) the analytical learner, (III) the common-sense learner, and (IV) the dynamic learner. Learners are capable of working in all four areas some of the time, but most of us tend to favor one style over all others. The trick for teachers is to provide experiences in the four areas to accommodate all learners and to increase their range of learning styles. It can be useful to view the model as a circle divided into four quadrants that can be used to guide lesson planning and teaching (see Figure 2.3).

♦ **Type I: The Imaginative Learner (Experiencing).** This type of learner seeks meaning. Type I learners are innovative and imaginative, preferring to learn through feeling and reflecting. Their teachers need to create a reason and provide a rationale for the learning that connects to their own lives and has relevance. Positive relationships and nurturing teachers are important aspects that need to be present in classrooms.

♦ **Type II: The Analytical Learner (Conceptualizing).** This type of learner seeks facts. Type II learners prefer to learn by watching and thinking. They create concepts and models. They appreciate information and teacher lectures.

♦ **Type III: The Common-Sense Learner (Applying).** This type of learner seeks usability and practical application and prefers to learn through thinking and trying out. Experimentation and problem solving are processes that intrigue this learner.

♦ **Type IV: The Dynamic Learner (Creating).** These learners seek to learn through trial and error and prefer to learn by trying out and sensing. They want to teach themselves and others and to use the teacher as a resource. They are risk takers and prefer self-discovery, disliking rigid routines and methodical tasks.

Silver, Strong, and Perini (2000) outline a model of four learning styles derived from the theories of Carl Jung and Isabel Briggs Myers:

♦ **Self-Expressive Learners.** These learners prefer opportunities for original, flexible, and elaborative thinking. They appreciate teachers who give them choices and facilitate their learning. They are innovative, creative learners.

♦ **Mastery Learners.** These learners prefer opportunities to observe, describe, memorize, and practice new learning to reach

Figure 2.3.   Learners tend to favor one particular learning style but are capable of working in all four areas as suggested by Bernice McCarthy's 4Mat Model (1990).

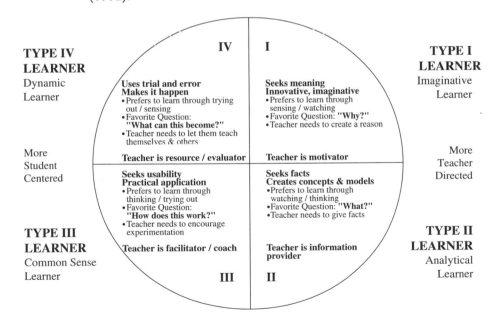

mastery. They appreciate teachers who present information and arrange for practice. They enjoy developing mastery of basic skills.

♦ **Understanding Learners.** These learners prefer opportunities to summarize, classify, compare, contrast, and look for cause and effect. They appreciate teachers who provide information and then probe for explanations and reasons behind the facts. They think logically and analytically, seeking evidence to support their learning.

♦ **Interpersonal Learners.** These learners prefer opportunities to socialize, describe feelings, empathize, and provide support and approval. They appreciate teachers who relate the content to them personally so that they can recognize relevance and add meaning to their work.

USING LEARNING AND THINKING STYLES IN THE CLASSROOM

The connections and similarities between and among these various learning styles can be compared using a matrix (see Figure 2.4). Vertically, each row outlines a different research interpretation. Horizontally, each column shows how the different perspectives align with each other.

Harvey Silver and colleagues often use metaphorical thinking in their workshops. The analogous use of four items with which most people are familiar (a beach ball, clipboard, microscope, and puppy) can help learners understand the attributes of each style and to remember that style by recalling those attributes that relate to the familiar items. Making students aware of these styles, perhaps by asking them about the attributes of Beach Balls, Clipboards, Microscopes, and Puppies, and having them brainstorm those characteristics will help students understand the differences of styles in the classroom.

After the brainstorming, students can link the profiles to what would be important to provide for these types of learners in the classroom in order for them to be successful in school. For example, Beach Balls would want to keep moving, be creative, and be free to go where they wish. Therefore if they were in a classroom at school, they would like choice and options in their learning and to have the opportunity to be creative and move freely, using centers and so forth. Students can rank these four items or symbols from 1 to 4, depending on their understanding of themselves. Teachers can point out that we all have some characteristics of each type but that students' top two choices show the way they would prefer to learn and the types of activities that would be most comfortable for them.

Teachers may want to take time to examine what each of the four symbols could appreciate in the classroom. One group of teachers generated the following list containing things that they thought the four types would value in the classroom:

Beach Ball

- Variety of resources
- Adaptive environment
- Various manipulatives
- Choice of activities
- Spontaneity
- Extensions to activities
- Personal freedom

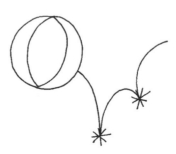

Clipboard

- Organization
- Structure
- Visual directions
- Clear closure
- Sequential learning
- Clear procedures
- Consistent routines
- Clear expectations

Microscope

- Discovery learning
- Analyzing concepts
- Deep exploration
- Discussions
- Focus on details
- Ownership

Puppy

- Comfortable environment
- Encouraging atmosphere
- Supportive grouping
- Safe climate
- Respectful colleagues
- Empathic listeners
- Sensitive peers

Figure 2.4. A matrix of learning styles illustrates their connections and similarities.

	Gregorc	Kolb	Silver/Strong/Hanson	4Mat/ McCarthy
Beach Ball	**Concrete Random** • Divergent • Experiential • Inventive	**Accommodator** • Likes to try new ideas. • Values creativity, flexibility and risk takers.	**Self Expressive** • Feelings to construct new ideas. • Produces original and unique materials.	**Type 4 Dynamic** . Create and act. . Usefulness and application of learning.
Clipboard	**Concrete Sequential** • Task oriented • Efficient • Detailed	**Converger** • Values what is useful and relevant, immediacy, and organizing essential information.	**Mastery** • Absorbs information concretely, and processes step by step.	**Type 3 Common Sense** • Think and do. • Active, practical. • Make things work.
Microscope	**Abstract Sequential** • Intellectual • Analytical • Theoretical	**Assimilator** • Avid readers who seek to learn. • Patience for research. • Values concepts.	**Understanding** • Prefers to explore ideas and use reason and logic based on evidence.	**Type 2 Analytical** • Reflect and think. • Observers who appreciate lecture methods.
Puppy	**Abstract Random** • Imaginative • Emotional • Holistic	**Diverger** • Values positive, caring environments that are attractive, comfortable, and people-oriented.	**Interpersonal** • Appreciates concrete ideas and social interaction to process and use knowledge.	**Type 1 Imaginative** • Feel and reflect. • Create and reflect on an experience.

It is not as important which style delineator a teacher uses as it is that the teacher recognize the needs of each of the styles and design the learning so that the diverse clientele in the classroom have their needs satisfied.

MULTIPLE INTELLIGENCES

Howard Gardner's theory of multiple intelligences provides us with another frame through which we can observe students and understand how they learn and process information.

It is of the utmost importance that we recognize and nurture all of the varied human intelligences, and all of the combinations of intelligences. We are all so different largely because we all have different combinations of intelligences. If we recognize this, I think we will have at least a better chance of dealing appropriately with the many problems that we face in the world. (Gardner, 1983)

Gardner offers us eight ways of being smart:

1. Verbal/Linguistic: reading, writing, speaking, and listening

2. Logical/Mathematical: working with numbers and abstract patterns

3. Visual/Spatial: working with images, mind mapping, visualizing, drawing

4. Musical/Rhythmic: using rhythm, melody, patterned sound, song, rap, dance

5. Bodily/Kinesthetic: processing information through touch, movement, dramatics

6. Interpersonal: sharing, cooperating, interviewing, relating

7. Intrapersonal: working alone, self-paced instruction, individualized projects

8. Naturalist: spending time outdoors, sorting, classifying, noticing patterns

Teachers in classrooms have been not only recognizing the various intelligences that students possess but also consciously providing learning experiences that include more than the most frequently used verbal and logical intelligences. They consider the notion that when we want to "catch fish" we bait the hook with what the fish like, not what the fisherman likes. So in classrooms teachers should use a variety of teaching and learning strategies as "bait" that will appeal to the learners, not just to the teacher.

"Kidwatching" is one way of gathering data to build learning profiles for each student. Teachers and students need to know their strengths to enhance self-confidence as well as areas that need improvement so goal setting and metacognition can be implemented. Teachers and students may use checklists and questionnaires (see Figures 2.5 through 2.10) to gain insight into students' preferred areas of multiple intelligence.

"How Are You Intelligent?" (Figure 2.5) is a checklist that students and teachers may use to increase personal awareness and understanding of areas of strength, which will increase self-awareness and confidence, and to identify areas that they may need to target for growth. Students may check off the items that are most like themselves and then transfer that information to a bar graph, filling in one cube in each row for each item checked in each intelligence category. The bar graph can then be cut to create each student's Unique Individual Profile (Figure 2.6), which may be used to compare and contrast their profile with other students with whom they may be working (Fogarty & Stoehr, 1995). This helps students recog-

Figure 2.5. How Are You Intelligent?

VERBAL/LINGUISTIC INTELLIGENCE	INTRAPERSONAL INTELLIGENCE
• I like to tell jokes, tell stories or tales. • Books are important to me. • I like to read. • I often listen to radio, TV, tapes, or CDs. • I write easily and enjoy it. • I quote things I've read. • I like crosswords and word games.	• I know about my feelings, strengths, and weaknesses. • I like to learn more about myself. • I enjoy hobbies by myself. • I enjoy being alone sometimes. • I have confidence in myself. • I like to work alone. • I think about things and plan what to do next.
LOGICAL/MATHEMATICAL INTELLIGENCE	**VISUAL/SPATIAL INTELLIGENCE**
• I solve math problems easily. • I enjoy math and using computers. • I like strategy games. • I wonder how things work. • I like using logic to solve problems. • I reason things out. • I like to use data in my work to measure, calculate, and analyze.	• I shut my eyes and see clear pictures. • I think in pictures. • I like color and interesting designs. • I can find my way around unfamiliar areas. • I draw and doodle. • I like books with pictures, maps, and charts. • I like videos, movies, and photographs.
INTERPERSONAL INTELLIGENCE	**BODILY/KINESTHETIC INTELLIGENCE**
• People ask me for advice. • I prefer team sports. • I have many close friends. • I like working in groups. • I'm comfortable in a crowd. • I have empathy for others. • I can figure out what people are feeling.	• I get uncomfortable when I sit too long. • I like to touch or be touched when talking. • I use my hand when speaking. • I like working with my hands on crafts/hobbies. • I touch things to learn more about them. • I think of myself as well coordinated. • I learn by doing rather than watching.
MUSICAL/RHYTHMIC INTELLIGENCE	**NATURALIST**
• I like to listen to musical selections. • I am sensitive to music and sounds. • I can remember tunes. • I listen to music when studying. • I enjoy singing. • I keep time to music. • I have a good sense of rhythm.	• I enjoy spending time in nature. • I like to classify things into categories. • I can hear animal and bird sounds clearly. • I see details when I look at plants, flowers, and trees. • I am happiest out doors. • I like tending to plants and animals. • I know the names of trees, plants, birds, and animals.

nize that together they have at least three or four areas of strength and therefore more tools for creativity and problem solving. This activity reinforces the notion that our diversity is our strength. As students learn through experience and reflection on those experiences, their profiles will be forever changing (see also Chapman, 1993).

Observing students as they work and interact helps us to know them better. Some classroom teachers set up areas where students choose games or activities for leisure time at noon hour or recess. The types of games they choose gives teachers information about their preferences. For example, some students choose games or activities that involve words and letters, others problems and logic, others creative options, and still others social interaction. Teachers often use clipboards and self-sticking notes to capture observations about students that can be transferred into student profiles (Figure 2.7) whenever possible.

Figure 2.6. What Is Your Unique Multiple Intelligences Profile?

Word Smart							
Math Smart							
People Smart							
Music Smart							
Self Smart							
Picture Smart							
Body Smart							
Nature							

SOURCE: Adapted by permission of Skylight Professional Development from page 57 of *Integrating Curricula with multiple intelligences: Teams, themes, and threads* by Robin Fogarty and Judy Stoehr. © 1995 IRI/Skylight Training and Publishing, Inc. www.skylightedu.com.

The use of logs and journals in which students reflect on their learning and their enjoyment or preference of one learning activity over another gives teachers information to build into student profiles. Having students use exit passes as they leave the class can give the teacher immediate feedback on specific topics. Just asking students what they enjoyed, or learned best from, or didn't appreciate, gives information that can be valuable in future planning. Teachers can also check for clarification and understand-

Figure 2.7. Teachers can capture observations over time about students' multiple intelligences and transfer them to student profiles.

STUDENT PROFILE	

Observing over time . . .   Name:

Verbal/Linguistic	Intrapersonal
Logical/Mathematical	Visual/Spacial
Interpersonal	Bodily/Kinesthetic
Musical/Rhythmic	Naturalist

ing of material that was examined in class that day by asking what was clear, what was unclear, or what questions still need clarification. Figure 2.8 offers a self-reflection tool that students can use in journals as a whole or as individual items over several days.

In early elementary classrooms, students can use symbols or a "Yes-Maybe-No" checklist (see Figure 2.9) instead of words to indicate their preferences. The teacher may pose questions like those listed on the bottom half of the checklist, and after thinking about each question the students can draw a face on the appropriate line that shows how they feel about the activity.

Figure 2.8. Eight Intelligences: Self-Reflection Tool Used by Students Individually or With Peers

Complete this page and compare your answers with your partner.

If I could do anything I like, I'd . . . .

Usually, when I have free time I . . . .

My hobbies are . . . .

At school I like to . . . .

The type of things that we do in class I really like are . . . .

I am uncomfortable when people ask me to . . . .

Do you like to work alone or with a group? Why?

As teachers become more aware of students' unique learning styles and intelligences, they become more able to design learning experiences that appeal to their students' different needs and interests. Because teachers are also unique individuals who tend to have styles of teaching that fit their personal profiles, it is often a stretch to include instructional and assessment tools and strategies that are not in their personal comfort zone.

Figure 2.9. Yes–Maybe–No Line

1.
2.
3.
4.
5.
6.
7.
8.
9.
10.

Ask students about a variety of activities that they might have the opportunity to do.

How do you feel about . . .

1. Drawing and artwork?
2. Musical activities?
3. Working with others?
4. Working alone?
5. Using numbers?
6. Writing? Talking?
7. Dancing, sports, moving while learning?
8. Solving problems?
9. Reading?
10. Thinking about things?
11. Working with technology?
12. Being a leader?

Teachers need to build a repertoire that will engage more learners and honor the diversity in each classroom. The Multiple Intelligences offer many options for including all eight where appropriate in lessons (see Figure 2.10). If a variety of multiple intelligence processes are used, they offer diverse learners more opportunities to learn and to show what they know in many ways.

Teachers continually gather data and observe students as the students become more familiar with their unique ways of learning. Teachers then can consciously include a variety of learning and assessment experiences that would appeal and engage a greater number of students. Students will then feel challenged in areas they feel confident in pursuing. We realize that with individual learning styles and multiple intelligence profiles, one size of learning could not possibly fit everyone in the classroom. Knowing the learners and consciously and strategically planning to address their styles, intelligences, and learning preferences will increase the chances of engaging them and offering a variety of ways to learn.

Figure 2.10. Suggestions for Using the Eight Multiple Intelligences

MUSICAL RHYTHMIC

Sing it
Create a beat
Rap it
Make a cheer
Create a jingle
Hum it
Identify sounds
React to sounds
Listen to sounds
Connect to music
Write a poem

VERBAL LINGUISTIC

Read it
Spell it
Write it
Listen to it
Tell it
Recall it
Use "you" words
Apply it
Chunk information
Say it
Discuss it
Use mnemonics

LOGICAL MATHEMATICAL

Make a pattern
Chart it
Sequence it
Create a mnemonic
Analyze it
Think abstractly
Think critically
Use numbers
Prove it
Interpret the data
Use the statistics

VISUAL SPATIAL

Mind maps
Graphic organizers
Video
Color code
Highlight
Shape a word
Interpret a graphic
Read a chart
Study illustrations
Visualize it
Make a chart
Create a poster

Multiple Intelligences
"Making Learning Palatable"

BODY KINESTHETIC

Role play
Walkabout
Dance
Lip sync
Skits/charades/mime
Construction
Math manipulatives
Sign language
Sports
Activity centers
Body language

INTERPERSONAL

Think-Pair-Share
Jigsaw
Cooperative grouping
Drama
Debates
Class meetings
Role play
Meeting of minds
Peer counseling
Tutors/buddies
Shared journals
Giving feedback

INTRAPERSONAL

Metacognition
Use self-talk
Work independently
Solve it your own way
Understand self
Journal it
Rehearse it
Use prior knowledge
Connect it
Have ownership

NATURALIST

Label it
Categorize it
Identify it
Form a hypothesis
Do an experiment
Adapt it
Construct it
Classify it
Investigate it
Discern patterns

SOURCE: Adapted from *Test Success in the Brain Compatible Classroom* (Chapman & King, 2000) and from presentation materials by Gayle Gregory (1998).

Assessing **3** the Learner

Just as one size of learning doesn't fit all, one size of assessment doesn't suit either. We can hold up clothing to see how it might look, but until we put it on we don't know what changes need to be made. We may need a new size or a different style or color. So in assessing the learning, we need different approaches to check the fit and adjust the learning.

We in education tend to banter about the terms *assessment, evaluation,* and *grading* without necessarily having clearly distinctive definitions for each term. *Assessment* is often referred to as the gathering of data, *evaluation* is the judging of merits, and *grading* is assigning values to letters or numbers for reporting purposes (Rolheiser, Bower, & Stevahn, 2000).

Assessment as ongoing feedback is a necessary component of the learning process, not something that happens at the end of the learning. It has been said that feedback is often too little, too late, too vague, presented in the wrong form, and therefore lacking in impact (Jensen, 1998a, p. 54). Our challenge is to find ways to facilitate ongoing feedback for students that will increase their chances to continue to grow and improve their learning.

One of the first things that needs to be done is pre-assessment to find out what students already know or can do.

It takes time to do quality pre-assessments, but it can be a very worthwhile process. Planning for individual needs is easier when one knows what a student knows, how the student feels about the topic, and what he or she is interested in learning about during the study.

PURPOSES OF PRE-ASSESSMENT

To find out

✓ What the student already knows about the unit being planned

✓ What standards, objectives, concepts and skills the individual student understands

✓ What further instruction and opportunities for mastery are needed

✓ What requires reteaching or enhancement

✓ What areas of interests and feelings are in the different areas of the study

✓ How to set up flexible groups: T-total, A-alone, P-partner, S-small group

When teaching with high achievement as a goal, one important aspect of assessing learners is finding out what the students already know. This knowledge is based on their prior learning and experiences. By doing a pre-assessment of knowledge, teachers can plan curriculum and design instruction to meet the needs of the total class as well as individuals. The written tests are one form of pre-assessment.

Try this handy tip! Administer the pretest 2 or 3 weeks before the information is to be taught. The test needs to vary in types of questions for an accurate assessment. That gives the teacher time to plan for the novice to the expert and those along the way. By administering the test early, the seeds of excitement have been planted about all the interesting things the students will be learning. Students need to realize that through experiences one learns. People may be at a novice level of knowing because of lack of experience and opportunity. This is sometimes difficult for a student to admit. One must realize that the pre-assessment tools provide information for planning what the individual needs and that no one is expected to be at the expert level in everything being taught.

When learners know the information, they may be allowed to move on to another dimension of the unit of study. For those who have not had exposure to the information prior to the pre-assessment, this allows the teacher to provide an experience for them.

One way to get this point across to students is to name some sports, hobbies, or free-time favorites and find those who are experienced and those who do not know much about them. These students have other areas of interests and expertise. We are all smart, just in different ways. For instance, a star football player knows all the plays of the game and practices for hours. There are some of us who attend the football games who know the basic rules, and then there are others who do not know anything about the game of football. This has nothing to do with their intelligence; this is their experience, their talents, their interests, and being in the right place at the right time.

Some children in first grade may be having difficulty with the concepts for adding and subtracting numbers. Yet when you get to the money unit you find that they have been going to the store, spending money, and getting change. These children are in fact able to use the principles of adding and subtracting. Experience and survival have taught them this. Other students may not have had these same experiences.

Components to consider as part of the pre-assessments:
If a pretest,

♦ Cover whole unit of study

♦ Include simple to complex and concrete to abstract understandings

♦ Chunk test questions in groupings that relate to the same standards so that the data when examined will clearly indicate knowledge or gaps in knowledge

♦ Recall facts

♦ Ask students to use the information to show another way, form, or situation

♦ Interpret information such as charts and graphs

♦ Allow drawing, interpreting, or demonstrating.

♦ Ask open-ended questions to elicit more information

More informally,

♦ Demonstrate with manipulatives, if appropriate, to show application

♦ Use interest surveys

♦ Use dialogue to find out what students want to learn and how they feel about the topic

♦ Analyze the pretest data so you can make planning decisions.

Rank scores to find

1. Appropriate uses of flexible grouping

2. Time lines for the unit of study or topic

3. Number of students at different levels of mastery

The teacher is then able to identify and determine which standards, concepts, and skills individuals have

✓ Beyond expectation (understand, apply, can transfer to other situations)

✓ Mastered (a basic understanding)

✓ That are approaching mastery

✓ At an introductory, novice, or beginning stage

Then a plan can be developed for each level of mastery.

There are other effective tools and strategies to use to pre-assess students' knowledge. Emotions and feelings play a large role in the way a student learns information. When a person has had a bad experience in the past and is learning or doing something that triggers that memory, there is a barrier formed that inhibits the new learning. When the experience is a quality one with purpose, positive impact, and a great experience, the learner feels open to learning more and experiencing more with the topic. These pre-assessment tools relate feelings, emotional links, and knowledge gathered from past experiences. This can have strong impacts on the present learning. The following are some examples to use as more informal pre-assessment tools that can be used at the beginning of lessons to open mental files and find out students' predispositions.

PRE-ASSESSMENTS

Squaring Off

This very successful pre-assessment tool involves the total group.

1. Place a card in each corner of the room with one of the following words or phrases that are effective ways to group according to learner knowledge:

Rarely ever	Sometimes	Often	I have it!
Dirt road	Paved road	Highway	Yellow brick road

2. Tell the students to go to the corner of the room that matches their place in the learning journey.

3. Participants go to the corner of the room that most closely matches their own learning status and discuss what they know about the topic or event and why they chose to go there.

Boxing

1. Getting to the Heart of the Matter

   Draw a box in the center of a piece of paper. Draw a smaller box inside the first box.
   - Outside Box:
     What do I know?

   - Inside Box:
     What do I want to learn?
     or
     What is my goal?

2. Gift of Success

   - Outside Box: *Write one of the following:*
     What else do I know about this topic?
     How does it fit?
     What does this have to do with _____?

   - Inside Box:
     Draw a model, picture
     Create Graphic Organizer to explain the topic

   - Middle of the Box:
     Summarize: What does that say?

Yes/No Cards

   ♦ Students make each set of cards. They write YES on one and NO on the other. They may use the back and front of one piece of paper, or they may have a piece of paper for each word.

   ♦ When a question is asked the students hold up YES or NO.

   1. Ask the students if they know the following vocabulary words and what they mean.

   2. Call out a word. Ask someone who has a YES card showing to check it out to make the students realize that you will be asking if they say YES.

Suggestion: Keep reminding them that if they do not know these words, these are some of the things they are going to be learning

♦ Ask a question from the unit that they will be studying. If they know they hold up YES, if not the NO card. Use some of the most interesting information so that it builds up the desire to learn more about the topic.

Suggestion: Sometimes a third card is needed: "some" or "often."

♦ Use plus (yes) and minus (no) signs for variation

♦ Got It! (yes); Not a Clue (no)

Graffiti Fact

Create a "Graffiti Board of Facts." Post all the things the class knows about the topic of study.

♦ What we knew.

♦ What we learned.

♦ What we want to learn next.

Suggestions:

1. Let students answer the question alone at first and jot down their answer.

   Why? This gives processing and thinking time. Also, everyone is engaged in answering the question.

2. Allow students to write their own responses to be posted.

   Why? This creates ownership to the answer.

ASSESSMENT TOOLS TO USE DURING THE LEARNING

As students are working we need to offer opportunities for feedback from teachers, from peers, and through self-reflection. Without feedback, people cannot improve. If we wait until the end of the learning it may be too late and incorrect information or skills may have been developed. The following strategies are engaging ways to assess student progress informally throughout the learning process.

Thumb It

Have students respond with the position of their thumb to get an assessment.

Where am I now in my understanding of _____?

a. Upside   b. Onside (sideways)   c. Downside

Know a lot about this   Know some   Know very little

Fist of Five

Show the number of fingers on a scale, with 1 being lowest and 5 the highest.

How well do I know this?

1   2   3   4   5

5. I know it so well I could explain it to anyone.

4. I can do it alone.

3. I need some help.

2. I could use more practice.

1. I'm only beginning.

Face the Fact

Happy   Straight   Sad

1. State a fact related to the topic that can be answered with an emotion.

2. Draw a Happy Face, a Straight Face, and a Sad Face on individual cards.

3. Hold up the card that matches the emotion.

4. Make motions with your hands to imitate the facial emotions.

5. Curve up for the happy face, flat for the straight face, or curve down for the sad face.

Reaching for the Top

1. Tell the students to extend one arm straight up in the air.

2. Move the opposite hand up that arm as if it were a gauge marked with a 1-to-5 scale. Number 1 is at the shoulder, number 3 is at the elbow, and number 5 is where the fingers are pointed to the ceiling.

As the student positions his hand against the upraised arm, the teacher can do a quick scan of the class to check for understanding.

Speedometer Reading

1. Think of the speedometer going from the 0-mph take-off to speeding at 100 mph

2. Lay one arm on top of the other with hands touching elbows

3. Move the arm that's on top from 0 mph to 100 mph to show how well you understand.

REFLECTIONS AFTER THE LEARNING

These are informal reflections that can be conducted after the learning to encourage metacognition.

Wraparounds

1. Participants form a circle.

2. Each individual takes a turn telling . . .
    a. Something he will use from information or activities learned today
    b. Something he will remember from today
    c. A significant AHA! from this session

Talking Topic

1. Form A/B partners

2. A tells a fact to B

3. B gives another fact back

4. Partners keep swapping facts back and forth

Conversation Circles

Form a conversation circle with a group of three students. The following is a way to use circles to improve communication.

1. Individuals assume A, B, or C names

2. "A" starts talking and continues until given signal

3. "B" continues with the topic

4. Then "C" picks up the topic

5. Continue until there are no more fact or ideas to add to the topic

Donut

Draw a donut shape.

1. On the outside, write "I am learning."

2. On the inside, write "I know."

Rotation Reflection

1. Post charts around the room with a related topic written on each sheet.

2. Small groups gather at each location to give ideas and views on the chart topic.

3. A recorder fills in the charts with great ideas generated.

4. A signal is given for the groups to move to the next chart and respond to the topic.

5. Groups continue around the room, visiting each chart in turn and adding ideas.

6. The last group remains at the chart, consolidates information, and reports it to the large group.

Paper Pass

This activity uses several large pieces of chart paper.

1. Place a different subject heading at the top of each piece of paper.

2. Each group brainstorms and writes down what it knows about its topic.

3. The group passes the paper to another group.

4. The second group reads all that has been written.

5. The second group writes down what else it knows about the topic.

6. The second group passes the paper to other groups to add to the sheet.

7. The last group finds references for the statements.

8. Place a page number and/or source beside each reference.

9. Share and post all the papers.

More Ideas!

B	What I Brought
W	What I Want
L	Learnings for Me
S	Suggestions for Next Time
Q	Questions I Have
G	Guesses
P	Pluses
M	Minuses
I	Insights
R	Requests
F	Favorites
D	Dislikes
T	Teach Me!

Select the items from the above list that are appropriate. Create a Data Board, leaving room for feedback from the students in each section chosen. Students respond to the appropriate question, and their answers are posted. They can keep adding information to the board during the unit.

♦ Journaling: Students need time allotted to writing journal entries of their requests, comments, questions, and reflections

♦ Plotting data on a variety of Graphic Organizers

- Polls and interviews
- Conferences
- Performances
- Pre- and posttests
- Portfolios

Grand Finale Comment

Give students a task to do as they are leaving the class. This is the Grand Finale Comment. These comments can give the teacher feedback about the learning AHAs, the difficulties according to the groups or individuals, and feelings about the situations. Some examples of these are listed below.

Individual Student

- Today I learned . . . Tomorrow I need . . .
- Today I felt . . . because . . .
- I would color today [color] because . . .
- I hope we . . . next.
- One word to describe today is . . .
- I felt like a [animal] during the . . . because . . .

Group

- Our group was great today when we . . .
- Tomorrow we are going to . . .
- A theme song for our work today would be . . .

Think of other innovative ways for students to report what they know. Pre-assessment is the beginning that will bring successful endings to the learning journey.

Surveys at Work

Construct quality surveys. Teachers know the goal, the purpose, and the information is to be learned. Survey often because interests change as students grow. These tools will teach you so much about the learners in your classroom!

Sample Interest Survey Questions

	Rarely Ever	Sometimes	Most of the Time
1. I like to make up songs.			
2. I like to try things that are hard to do.			
3. Brain puzzles hold my interest.			
4. I like to take things apart and assemble them.			
5. I enjoy creating.			
6. I need manipulatives to learn.			
7. I am a follower.			
8. I am a leader.			
9. I prefer to work alone.			
10. I like to read.			
11. I prefer to work with others.			
12. I like to draw my own pictures.			
13. I can see visual images in my head.			
14. I have at least one pet.			
15. I enjoy animals.			
16. I would rather be outside than inside.			
17. I would rather be inside than outside.			
18. I like school.			
19. I do not like school.			

20. School would be better if _____.

21. If I have free time I prefer to

    a. _____

    b. _____

    c. _____

22. I do not like _____ because _____.

23. Additional Comments

    a. _____

    b. _____

Sample Unit Interest Survey

Focus: Study of a country

- ◆ History
- ◆ Industry
- ◆ Beliefs
- ◆ Government
- ◆ Celebrations, festivals, holidays, and rites
- ◆ Geography and location

ONGOING ASSESSMENT

In classrooms everywhere, teachers are using authentic strategies to teach the standards. They also use authentic tools to assess the standards, matching the learning to the assessment. For example, when students work on a project, they are assessed on their work throughout the development of the project as well as on their final report on the project.

Usually a rubric is developed and used throughout the entire process so that the student, the parents, and the teacher understand the criteria and expectations and can assess progress along the way.

Portfolios also are now used in many classes, with teachers relating that the portfolios are being used as vehicles for reflection, ongoing conversations, and goal setting between and among students, teachers, and parents.

PORTFOLIOS

What Are They?

Portfolios are collections of student work for specific purposes based on criteria that support and provide evidence of application and understanding of the targeted concepts or skills. They can identify progress, show evidence of success, support evaluation and grading, and contain pieces that show what additional learning needs to take place. They are a way of facilitating ongoing feedback and reflection during the learning process.

Why Do We Use Them?

Richard Stiggins (1993) suggests that a portfolio is like a color video with sound, much more vivid than just a test paper. It gives a much fuller picture and provides supportive evidence to substantiate the feedback or grade that has been given. It also encourages student ownership and reflection on progress toward learning goals. Portfolios contain evidence of growth with initial samples of work and pieces added periodically to show progress. Part of the portfolio process is the ongoing dialogue about quality and criteria that occurs between and among the teacher, students, and peers. They enable students to reflect on their work and to analyze quality and set goals.

How Do We Use Them?

Often, the portfolio is a partnership, with both the teacher and student being involved in selecting pieces to put in the portfolio. Often, the teacher will set criteria for selection and allow several choices to be made by the students. Some teachers use colored dots to identify pieces that are included: red dot on student selected pieces, yellow dot on teacher selected, and green dot on teacher/student selected pieces. There can be four steps in the portfolio process: Collect, Select, Reflect, and Project (Burke et al., 1993).

Collect

Pieces are gathered from the beginning of the year or unit based on criteria. They may include homework, projects, written pieces, mind maps, tests, assignments, cassettes or videos, letters, graphic organizers, lab reports, poems, raps, audiotapes, and book reviews.

Evidence in the portfolio may be varied depending on the subject area.

Portfolios tell a story . . . put in anything that helps tell the story.
(Paulson & Paulson, 1991, p. 1)

Select

Students select pieces based on guidelines. The criteria may include

♦ Best piece/something I'm proud of

♦ Work in progress

♦ Student/teacher selection

♦ Most improved/difficult piece

♦ Special or free choice

Every so often students will examine the pieces and decide which ones should stay in the collection and which should be deleted. Pieces may be deleted because

♦ There is enough evidence of that competency already

♦ It doesn't really show what is needed

♦ A new piece is superior

Reflect

The student will then write a reflection to be attached to the piece that explains why it was selected, what criteria it satisfies. Over time, students add other pieces that may show growth from the last item or can replace others. Not all pieces are necessarily the best effort but may be included as baseline evidence to show growth in the future.

Project

Reflections and examination of items can lead to goal setting. Students can decide what to do next, what to focus on, what needs improvement, what to celebrate.

Portfolio conferences are effective ways to share student growth with others. Students articulate their learning and goal setting to colleagues, parents, and significant others.

Each student is an individual, and each portfolio will be unique to each learner, showing the individuality and growth of the learner.

GRADING

Teachers tend to give grades for many different reasons. There seems to be no commonly accepted yardstick for student achievement. Opinions about what should be evaluated and what actually is evaluated are aspects of ongoing dialogue among educators. Grades are often given to

1. Measure content mastery—to show what the student knows in the subject area

2. Chart progress—to communicate progress on individual goals and show the working level on a specific content

3. Motivate students—to prod the student to work harder or to reward the student for trying and giving so much effort

4. Provide information to a variety of audiences—students turn in their grades for recognition, awards, scholarships, and admittance into colleges and universities

Grades are not the only tools teachers use for their final evaluation of what students have learned. Ongoing assessments have been giving feedback all during the unit of study, and there are several possible class scenarios for the final evaluation:

♦ Give the common posttest to compare the pre- and postperformance. This is the same test given as the pre-assessment. The comparison of pre- and posttest may show progress or competence or lack of progress. If there are skills or content that requires more practice, the teacher will need to plan for that to happen. The results could also show areas of weakness for further study. Posttests will determine if students are knowledgeable, have improved, and have enduring understanding or need further practice for mastery to be acquired.

♦ Develop a test that evaluates the material studied by the different groups in the adjusted assignments. This test is based on the level of complexity of the study. Some of the questions would be on all tests. These questions would come from the information presented to the total group throughout the study. With this instrument, the groups of students would be given a written test consisting of the material the individual groups had studied. This system allows teachers to communicate students' achievements on the specific information that they have been studying. They are not being compared with the students working on a less challenging or more difficult area of the study.

♦ Some evaluation instruments combine both scenarios. There are questions given to all the students, and then a portion of the test is developed specifically to address an individual student or group of students. All the above scenarios are examples of written tests given at the end of a section of study. They may not stand alone as a final grade. The written test grade may be only one piece of the data that compiles the final grade. Evidence and grades have been gathered throughout to show a true picture of the student's performance.

AUTHENTIC TASKS

An authentic task asks students to perform tasks in a realistic, real-world context (Wiggins & McTighe, 1998). This may be part of an instructional activity, such as a demonstration, a presentation, or a role-playing event. The students are asked to demonstrate mastery in ways that are of interest to them. Therefore, the knowledge mastery is shown or demonstrated in a way the student can convey it best.

Assessments for Authentic Performances

Examples of assessment tools include rubrics, anecdotal notes, checklists, journal entries, samples of student work, self-evaluation, and conferences. These tools would be used to assess various types of learning activities from role-playing to projects. Learning needs to be the goal, but making the appropriate grade is often the main focus. Conveying an accurate portrait of students as learners is a complex task.

For example, students are asked to work a problem in math. Then they might be asked to draw the problem and then explain the problem to someone else. In reading, students might be asked to read about a character at a certain point in the text. Then they might be asked to draw the character and put the character in the setting described in the text. Another time they could be asked to role-play that character or find the background music to depict the character's feelings during a particular part of the story.

These are authentic strategies that allow the learner to interpret meaning. Some of these could be assessed with a written form but most would need an authentic assessment tool to match the authentic task.

The following is a list of tasks and products that teachers can use to assess student learning in more authentic ways:

♦ Make a mural

♦ Plan a trip

- Conduct a panel
- Create a magazine
- Develop a display
- Create a talk show about . . .
- Choreograph a dance
- Create costumes
- Draw a comic strip
- Teach a lesson
- Create a flow chart
- Design a video
- Complete a portfolio
- Write lyrics for a song
- Design a survey and interview
- Conduct a demonstration
- Illustrate a story
- Create a puppet play
- Design a bulletin board
- Create a time line on the computer
- Role-play the story
- Write a persuasive article
- Develop a new innovation to . . . .

Clear expectations and criteria need to be communicated up front so that students know the target and work toward it.

For a more accurate report, a teacher includes a grade, a portfolio to show the evidence to support the grade, a comment section with specific data about individual performance, and a parent conference for students and teachers to discuss areas of needs and areas of mastery.

Student Choices

Teachers are experimenting with a variety of ways to allow students to show what they know. One teacher has been quite creative in designing tests. She offered the students two options. The first option was traditional, consisting of 20 right and wrong answers to volume and area problems with memorized formulas and no calculator. Points were given for correct formula, answer, and label of answer. The second option allowed calculator use and a formula sheet for students during the test. The problems were applications to real life, thus not perfect math numbers. The shapes were real ice cream cones or lawn sprinklers and showed the actual uses of formulas in our everyday lives.

The second option involved in-depth thinking and multiple-step problems, and it allowed some room for alternate answers. The teacher reported that several students were quite excited about having a choice. Several were hesitant, not knowing which was the best test for them to show what they knew. Several had difficulty figuring out why the teacher might give partial credit for a wrong answer.

FINAL GRADES

Many agendas influence the final grade. Some capable students do not work very hard but still receive an A. Other students apply themselves and work diligently to do their best but still do not get an A. Grades can motivate as well as show evidence of performance and acquired knowledge, but they also can be demoralizing. Comments need to be made that clarify the effort or lack of effort made by each student. A strong work ethic is one of the competencies listed under Self-Motivation in Goleman's Emotional Intelligences. Teachers need to honor persistence, tenacity, and effort.

Tomlinson (1995) suggests that some teachers give students a grade based on their success on the material they were studying. An identifying code can tell the parent that this grade was given at the student's level to show competency and not for comparison with the rest of the class. Thus a student might get an A working at his own level but a D in comparison to classmates.

As we move to a more differentiated classroom, we need to communicate with parents, students, and the broader community so that they understand our intentions and the changes that are taking place. When they comprehend, they will support the processes that are best for students.

As learning tasks need to be differentiated, so do assessment strategies so that all learners get to learn in a variety of ways and show what they know in ways that are comfortable, durable, and "suit" the learner.

Adjusting, **4**
Compacting,
and Grouping

When we design clothes for people we consider their height, weight, and shape because those things influence the size of the clothing. As we know, not every student wears the same size, and of course we don't force them into a size Small when they need a Large. Not every student has the same background and experience and so is not necessarily as knowledgeable or skillful in every topic or skill as other students. We also know that we may get tired of wearing the same old thing, and students get tired of the "same old thing" in the classroom, too. Yet we often force them to endure the same lesson (in the same format) whether they already know the content or haven't any idea what is going on. This is why adjustments need to be made in their learning.

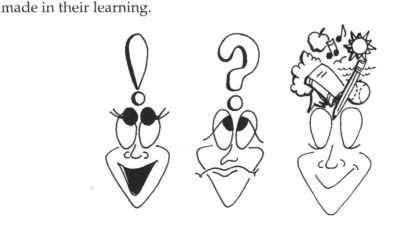

ADJUSTABLE ASSIGNMENTS: WHAT ARE THEY?

In classrooms everywhere we are examining how we can get a better fit for all students. Adjustable assignments allow teachers to help students focus on essential skills and understanding key concepts, recognizing that they may be at different levels of readiness. Some may or may not be able to handle different levels of complexity or abstraction. Although the assignment is adjusted for different groups of learners, the standards, concepts, or content of each assignment have the same focus and each student has the opportunity to develop essential skills and understanding at his or her appropriate level of challenge. The activities better ensure that students explore ideas at their level while building on prior knowledge and experiencing incremental growth.

Why Do We Use Them?

Using adjusted assignments allows students to begin learning where they are and to work on challenging and worthwhile tasks. If we were growing flowers and some of the seeds had sprouted and were ready to flower, we would not pull them out by the roots and make them start again from seed. It sounds a bit bizarre when we think about it. We of course would give the plants that were advanced in their growth the light, water, and food they need and would nurture the seedlings that were just sprouting to help them bloom and grow. Adjusting assignments allows for reinforcement or extension of concepts based on student readiness, learning styles, and/or multiple intelligence preferences. Appropriate adjustments in the learning have a greater chance of providing a "flow" experience in which each student is presented with challenging work that just exceeds his or her skill level.

This also increases the chances of success for each learner because that success is within reach, and ultimately success will be highly motivating. Adjusting assignments also decreases the chances of "downshifting" and the sense of helplessness that students feel when a challenge is beyond their capabilities.

How Do We Use Them?

Initially, as in any planning process, the concepts, skills, and content that will be the focus of the activity are identified and aligned with targeted standards and expectations.

Using some method of pre-assessment (quizzes, journal entries, class discussions and data collection techniques, learning profiles, etc.), teachers gather data to determine the prior knowledge of students for the new content or the skill that is targeted for learning. The pre-assessment data are compiled. Then the key standards and concepts to be taught during the unit are determined. The teacher then decides which parts of the study should be taught to the total class and how they will be presented. The appropriate places to teach these concepts and/or skills are determined. Then comes the time to make decisions about any adjustable assignment. Assignments are adjusted to meet the needs of learners based on their present knowledge or skill level. The following are questions the teacher will answer when making decisions about these assignments.

♦ What content does each of the groups already know?

♦ What does each group need to learn?

♦ What strategies should be used to facilitate the learning of each portion?

♦ What is the most effective way to group for each activity?

♦ What assessment tools will be used so that students will be accountable?

♦ Are the plans meeting the individual needs of the students?

Basic knowledge and experience varies among learners so adjustable assignments may be needed. Here is an example that is typical of what teachers face every time they start planning for all of their students.

Example: Adjustable Assignments for Early Elementary Grades

The Money Unit

Figure 4.1, Part A, shows what the groups of students know and can do based on the pre-assessment data analysis. This does not show numbers in the group but the knowledge or skill the group has. Part B is completed with tasks, assignments, or lessons that students require to continue their learning and understanding.

Part A: Advanced Mastery. Students know the names of the coins. They can count their money and make accurate change. They are consumer-wise as far as using money to purchase goods. Some of these students have been shopping in the neighborhood stores. Therefore they have the background knowledge base. Other students will need those basics before they can proceed. Real-life experiences have taught the content. Therefore these students need to work with elements of money other than the basics.

Figure 4.1. Adjustable Assignments: Money

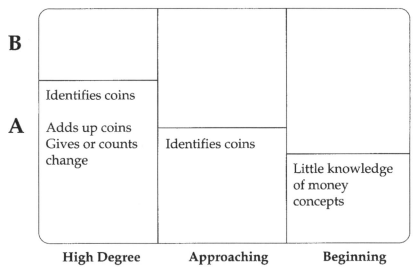

Standard: To be able to use currency in daily situations
Content: Coins

Part A: Approaching Mastery. These students have shown that they know the names of the coins. They are limited as far as the other concepts being taught. Therefore they need to begin counting and adding up coins and working with different combinations of money. As they advance, they can move to purchasing and receiving or giving change.

Part A: Beginners. This group of students shows that they know few if any of the names of the coins or their worth. They will need all of the information taught so that they develop a knowledge base. Because of adjustable assignments, all of these groups will be challenged and will learn information using a variety of strategies based on their needs. The students will work in groups that are designed to meet their needs. There will be ongoing assessment throughout the learning to provide appropriate feedback and to adjust assignments further.

As a result of this information, the teacher designed three meaningful activities at the levels the three groups needed.

The more advanced group (a high degree of mastery) worked at running a snack shop for recess and lunch. They priced the snacks and sold them, making change and counting the cash to calculate their earnings. They also used calculators to check their work.

During class time these students engaged in activities that led them further in their understanding of coins and their relationship to each other. Using actual coins at a center, the students challenged one another with combinations. "I have ten coins that make a dollar," said Pat. "That's ten dimes," chimed in Tara. "I have six coins that make a dollar," said Corey. "That could be three quarters, two dimes, and a nickel," said Jodie. The game became quite competitive as pairs kept score of their successes.

They also used calculators to total amounts of items on their "wish lists" for birthday gifts.

The group that was able to recognize the coins (approaching mastery) used coin stamps to make patterns with their partners. They challenged other group members to identify coins and give the total. They collected discarded toys and items from home and priced them to create a class "garage sale." They priced the items and had a garage sale using money.

The group that needed more experience (the beginners) to recognize the coins played a coin game similar to Concentration, in which they had to be able to recognize the coins and match them. They also began to match equivalents such as five pennies and a nickel equaling a dime, or two nickels equaling a dime, and so on.

All students were able to "shop" at the snack shop and garage sale and practiced using coins appropriately. They also were integrated into the operation of the two sales and worked with more experienced students who modeled and added to their learning.

All students were engaged in interesting and challenging activities that added to their experience.

Figure 4.2 shows what that data may look like for a Spanish standard of everyday conversation and the topic of giving directions.

Section A shows what the three groups of students know and are able to do in relation to the standard and content. Section B would show what needs to be done to extend the learning for that group.

The Advanced Mastery group (only 4 students) went online and found street maps of Mexico City. They wrote directions to areas or points of interest and produced posters advertising the attributes of that location.

The Approaching Mastery group designed a board game that used the vocabulary of giving directions. They produced interesting adaptations of board games with which they were familiar and wrote task cards for the games using vocabulary beyond what they had used in the past, incorporating new terminology.

The Beginners group worked in pairs to give one another directions to various areas in the school. They drew task cards and were able to direct

Figure 4.2. Adjustable Assignments: Spanish.

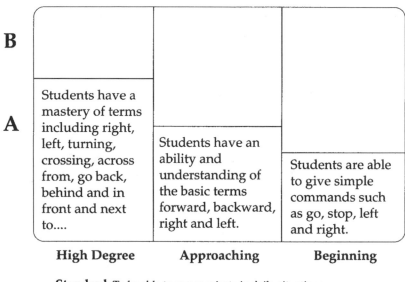

B

A Students have a mastery of terms including right, left, turning, crossing, across from, go back, behind and in front and next to....

Students have an ability and understanding of the basic terms forward, backward, right and left.

Students are able to give simple commands such as go, stop, left and right.

High Degree   **Approaching**   **Beginning**

Standard: To be able to communicate in daily situations
Content: Giving and following directions

one another to the cafeteria, office, or computer lab using Spanish. They then participated in a game similar to Twister in which they spun a wheel and followed the directions given.

More levels of readiness may be identified and adjusted if needed, but when first beginning this process, three levels may be complicated enough for the teacher to manage.

After the pre-assessment has been given, the teacher analyzes the data and plots them on the chart in Section A (Figure 4.3).

After the data have been entered, the teacher needs to consider what the students still need to know and be able to do to extend their learning. Teachers then fill in the B part of the grid with a learning that is suitably challenging and engaging in order to bring those learners to the next level. It may be a lesson, activity, task, or assignment. There may be different assignments that students do independently and that are given at two levels, in pairs, or in small groups, thus leaving the teacher free to interact and facilitate new content or processes with another group of students. The teacher may choose from a variety of curriculum approaches such as projects, centers, integration, or problem-based learning.

Figure 4.3. Adjustable Assignments Grid for Use by Teachers to Record Data About Student Readiness Levels

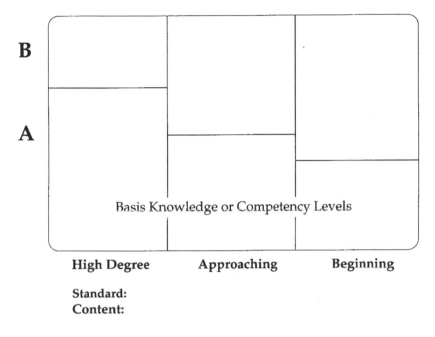

Note: This is not about number or time

CURRICULUM COMPACTING

What Is It?

Curriculum compacting is a strategy first shared by Joe Renzulli of the University of Connecticut (see also Tomlinson, 1999, 2001). It provides for the student who is very capable and knowledgeable in a particular topic in a subject area. It is a way of maximizing time for the more advanced learner.

Why Do We Use It?

Many students, because of prior experience, interests, and opportunities, may bring to the topic prior knowledge and skills that have been acquired over time. These may have been acquired through voracious reading, travel, and personal interest about a topic or from a mentor or role model who has had an influence on the learner. It is for these students that compacting may be used on occasion in order to enrich their curriculum, enhance and stretch their thinking, and help them develop into more self-directed learners. In many classrooms, where teaching to the "middle" is the norm, some learners are bored as they "repeat history," and others are lost because they don't have the background or experience they need to understand or be able to do what is expected of them. Compacting/enriching may be used with the high-end or advanced learner(s) identified after a pre-assessment is given. It is important to allow all learners to move at their own pace, thus creating the "relaxed alertness" that the Caines suggest. Challenging experiences that are perceived as "doable" in a learning situation put students into a state of "flow," thus engaging them at their level of challenge and not frustrating or boring them by giving them too difficult or too easy a task.

How Do We Do It?

Phase 1

In this phase, after an exploratory session where students are able to access prior knowledge and discuss their initial concepts and knowledge, a pre-assessment is given.

Figure 4.4. Curriculum Compacting Used to Provide Enrichment for Advanced Learners Beyond the Regular Curriculum

Phase 1	Phase 2 Analyze data	Phase 3
Exploratory Phase	**Mastery:** skills, concepts What have they mastered?	**Advanced Level Challenges**
Pre-assessment: • Test • Conference • Portfolio conference	**Needs to Master:** What else do they need to know?	• **Investigation** • **Problem Based Learning** • **Service Learning** • **Project** • **Contract**
To find out what the learner • Knows • Needs to know • Wants to know	**How will they learn it?** .Gain with whole class .Independent study .Homework .Mentor / buddy in or out of school .On-line learning	**Opportunities for** **Successful Intelligence** **Sternberg, 1996** • Analytical • Practical • Creative • **Assessment**

This may be in the form of:

♦ A pretest

♦ A conference where the learner shares knowledge and understanding about the topic

♦ A portfolio presentation in which students show evidence of their comprehension and skill level (any or all of these may be used)

Phase 2

After the pre-assessment, the teacher analyzes the data and identifies what the student already knows and has mastered and what the student still needs to learn.

This additional knowledge or skill may be acquired by:

♦ Joining the total class group for that concept or information

♦ Independent study

♦ Homework assignments

♦ Collaborating with a mentor or learning buddy in or outside school

♦ Online learning

Phase 3

Once the "missing pieces" have been added, the student(s) may choose or be offered

♦ An investigation or research project

♦ An ill-structured problem to solve

♦ A service learning opportunity

♦ A project

♦ A negotiated contract

♦ A special assignment

These assignments facilitate the challenge of applying their knowledge and skill in a practical and/or creative way. Robert Sternberg (1996), a noted psychologist, defines "successful intelligence" as including the aspects of being analytical, practical, and creative, not just knowing.

This allows learners to enhance their understanding and also obtain an added perspective on the subject matter. Compacting/enrichment is a strategy often used with academically gifted or talented students to enhance their curriculum. It may be done as a pullout or partial pullout model or orchestrated in the classroom with the subject teacher. If students are pulled out, they should not miss other subject areas of study that they have not mastered. Teachers must be sure that students really do have full mastery of the concept, not just surface-level knowledge. Students should not be required to complete the regular classroom assignments in the subject for which they have compacted out.

What Does It Look Like?

Some forms of compacting/enrichment take into consideration that some students have ample prior knowledge or experience to warrant a full semester or grade-level subject advancement. This would include the French student skipping first-year French because she is fluent in the language. Another example is a pre-algebra student skipping Algebra 1 and starting in Algebra 2.

Another scenario is the first grader going up with the third grade for reading each day.

Compacting/enrichment also occurs when students in several grade-level math classes are identified as being beyond curriculum expectations and so are pulled out of the classes during math time for enhanced or accelerated learning with an identified extension teacher.

COLLABORATIVE PLANNING MODELS

In some schools there are several teachers teaching the same grade level (such as four teachers teaching at third grade). Teachers in each class pre-assess the students in a math concept and cluster them by skill level into four new class groupings of advanced, competent, basic, and beginning (see Figure 4.5).

The four teachers collaborate to design learning experiences for each group. Each of the four teachers takes one of the groups during math time and facilitates the learning for that particular group.

This scenario encourages teacher collaboration to enhance the school's professional learning community. Teachers share resources, ideas, and strategies and further develop their repertoire of teaching through professional dialogue and problem solving. Common planning time may help facilitate this process. This could be used occasionally for special topics, and other math topics could be taught in regular classrooms.

In-Class Compacting/Enrichment

As shown in Figure 4.6, any class may divide into a number of groupings in relationship to mastery. There may be one or two, a few, or none of

Figure 4.5. Collaborative Jigsaw Compacting

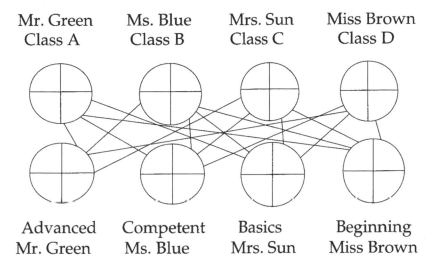

| Mr. Green | Ms. Blue | Mrs. Sun | Miss Brown |
| Class A | Class B | Class C | Class D |

| Advanced | Competent | Basics | Beginning |
| Mr. Green | Ms. Blue | Mrs. Sun | Miss Brown |

Figure 4.6. In-Class Compacting

C O M P A C T I N G	High degree of mastery	Approaching mastery	Beginning

Number of students in each group will vary depending on the topic or standard.

Curriculum compacting may be used for very advanced student(s). Often compacting is not required.

Figure 4.7. Personal Agenda to Keep Track of Time and Tasks

❀ ❀ ❀   A Personal Agenda   ❀ ❀ ❀

My Agenda (name): _____

Beginning on (date): _____

Dates:	Student Tasks	Log How I used my time:	Reflections	Completion Date Teacher & Student Sign-off

the students who need to have enrichment offered because of a high level of mastery.

Students may work alone, with a partner with similar interests, or in a small group of students focusing on the same materials and/or applications. This would depend on the number of students compacting and their interests and learning profiles. The teacher may want to have students develop an agenda to keep track of time and tasks (Figure 4.7). Students fill in the date and the task column of the agenda for the class, day, or unit of study. After each task is completed, they detail the progress in the log column and then chronicle their reflections in the next column. Each student and the teacher then conference and sign off in the last column.

They may use double-duty logs (Figure 4.8) to monitor steps and record reflections as they work on the assignment. This ongoing assessment helps both teacher and students clearly see the successes, progress,

---

Figure 4.8. Double-Duty Log

Double-duty logs allow students to record or list facts and information about content or process and then reflect on that information immediately or at another time to integrate it into their thinking and deepen their understanding. It allows students to process the information and make sense or meaning. It also facilitates revisiting the material to clarify or add to the thinking.

Facts or Ideas	Thoughts and Reflections

---

and needs throughout the assignment. It helps the students keep track of their time, reflect on their work, and set goals for the next step.

Adjusting and compacting are two techniques that strategic teachers use to help students get "a good fit" so they feel comfortable and capable in their learning. Most instructional strategies can be used to adjust the learning.

FLEXIBLE GROUPING

Finding the Right Size

Flexible grouping is often needed to facilitate differentiated instruction. Everyone has strong and weak areas of ability and interest. Students need to be placed in groups that maximize their instructional time based on their performance levels. Grouping flexibility allows students to move according to their demonstrated performance, interests, and varied knowledge base level. Students are grouped to meet their instructional, emotional, and personal needs. If a group of students gets along socially, they will usually meet the instructional expectations.

By remembering to use each component of TAPS in planning, the individual social needs have a greater chance of being met. These grouping methods can be used where they fit in the classroom. Some students can work well in all of these ways but every learner has preferences (Goleman, 1995).

A person who is very strong in their intrapersonal intelligence processes may prefer to solve problems better by working alone. He is able to solve the problem independently and does not see the need to work with a group. It takes time to think. Often this student will get really quiet in a group situation and become more metacognitve in order to process their learning.

Other students will be very strong in interpersonal intelligence. They are sometimes called "social butterflies." They feel the need to talk about concepts to understand them fully. They prefer to work with others rather than alone. These students bring empathy and harmony to the group.

Groups need

♦ Ample space to work

♦ Clear directions and procedures

♦ Rules and guidelines established

♦ Individual roles assigned for group responsibilities

♦ A time frame assigned for on-task work

♦ To tap into all members' strengths

Some students learn best while working alone; others work better when grouped with others. This offers students options designed to tap into different readiness levels, interests, talents, and learning modalities. An effective, quality pre-assessment helps decide which type of grouping will be the most effective for that particular part of the learning. Flexible grouping is in constant use and is forever changing in planning differentiated instruction.

Total Group

Alone

Partner

Small Group

TAPS (a rap)

Remember!

Some things need to be taught to the class as a whole.
There are certain things the Total Group should be told.

Working Alone, students get to problem-solve in their own way.
They will be in charge of what they think, do, and say.

With a Partner, many thoughts and ideas they can share.
They can work and show each other the solutions there.

Effective Small Groups work together to cooperate
Using the group's ideas and talents their learning
will accelerate.

So use a variety of ways to group students you see.
This TAPS into student's potential, as it should be.

GROUPING STRATEGIES

The following is a list of suggested ways to group students to meet their needs better.

Knowledge of a Subject

Cluster grouping of a small number of students within a heterogeneously grouped classroom can be used. This way the students are grouped according to their prior experiences and knowledge about the topic. A pre-assessment is given to determine what the students know at the beginning of the study. This allows each group to be given tasks that involve a variety of opportunities for novices as well as experienced students. When grouped in this manner, students are challenged and are interested in the work rather than being bored by information they already have experienced or frustrated by something they know nothing about.

For instance, in a science curriculum, one or more students might be very knowledgeable about the unit on creatures of the sea. These students are a valuable resource to the entire class in this area of high interest. They need to study and add to their knowledge base rather than review the information they already know. The next unit studied in the science class might be something that is unfamiliar to them, so they would need to acquire the basics and move in with a different group to study. The knowledge base of an individual is based on experiences. The novice or beginner needs more of the basic topic information than the experienced learner does.

Ability to Perform a Task or a Skill

Everyone has talents and skills that they can do better than others. One type of group to form would be the very skilled. Another might be those who are less skilled in a given area and need lots of help.

Still another would be forming teams of masters, those who do the subject well, and of apprentices, those who need one-on-one direction and assistance.

The purpose of ability grouping is so that the student can work with materials and information that is challenging and stimulating at a personal level. Assignments differ by making adjustments consisting of varying levels of difficulty. Questions are molded to pull information from students according to what they can comprehend. This fosters continued growth because one size does not fit all. Differentiated instruction accommodates academic diversity. Wagon Wheel Teaming, based on an idea developed by Sheila Silversides (in Kagan, 1992), can be used to group students quickly and randomly into groups of three or four that include a beginning-level student, two average-level students, and an expert-level student. As shown in Figure 4.9, four concentric circles are fastened in the center with a paper fastener so that they can rotate. The circles rotate to form new teams that include all three types of learners in each group.

Figure 4.9.   Wagon Wheel Teaming: Rotating Concentric Circles to Form Teams of Three or Four Learners at Different Levels

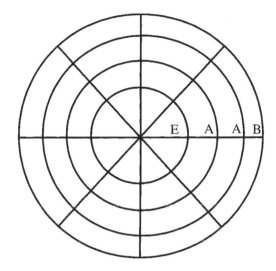

B is Beginning-level student
A is Average-level student
E is Expert-level student

Interests in a Specific Area of the Content

If a learner is interested in a topic or subject, the desire and emotions involved engage the learner. Conversations, interest surveys, and inventories give teachers information to weave this information into the learning. Why? By addressing what the learner is interested in, teachers have a link for the new learning. The desire to learn more is there. Students are interested in the arts, sports, games, role models, and outside activities that challenge their minds. In school, if their interests can be found, they are more likely to be engaged. Learning comes easier, and attention spans are longer on content that students are interested in learning.

Peer-to-Peer Tutoring

Having students assist each other with specific needs is a way to give them responsibility for understanding what they know and for how they can use the information. The student who is tutoring is gaining from this experience. If you teach something, you remember it and realize what you know and how you know it. The learner is gaining from the experience, too, because it is an individualized instruction that is tailored to a personal need. Students often communicate with each other using different words than the teacher would, and sometimes their way of explaining information may be easier for the peer to understand. Some examples are peer tutoring, peer reading, and peer journaling.

Cooperative Learning

Remember, if the people in a group get along socially, they will usually get the job done! Students learn social skills as well as cognitive skills and most often use higher levels of thinking as they discuss and clarify information. When using cooperative learning, the group comes to a consensus on a common goal or a specific assignment. Those in the group are assigned specific roles to play for a particular task. Both individual and group accountability is built in as an important part of a cooperative learning experience. Experts in cooperative group learning recommend that groups be structured heterogeneously.

Of great importance to this discussion are the Lou and others, (1996) findings that students of all ability levels benefit from ability grouping when compared with not grouping at all—students of low ability actually perform worse when they are placed [in] homogeneous groups with students of low ability—as opposed to students of low ability placed in heterogeneous groups. (Marzano, Pickering, & Pollack, 2000, p. 87)

For heterogeneous groupings that occur randomly, try using the grid called Stick Picks (Figure 4.10), based on an idea shared by public-school teacher W. Brenner (Fremont, CA).

Sharing Groups

Sometimes, teachers group students to share information, to research a topic, or for review purposes. Students can learn so much from each other. It can be very refreshing for students to hear information from many sources, in many voices. It also facilitates the opportunity for review and processing to reinforce and clarify ideas. It can provide movement that is important to the physical needs of some learners.

Sharing can be done with students standing, sitting on the floor, sitting around a table, rearranging desks, or creating other comfortable spaces conducive to conversations. Plot these throughout the curriculum for conversations, discussions, and teaching that make the students responsible for their learning. This gives ownership!

Figure 4.10. Stick Picks: Used to Create Random Groups of Heterogeneous Learners

By using sticks you can efficiently and quickly create random groups. As students enter the class, hand each one a stick. The following list shows you the colors to put on each stick. Number the sticks and use magic marker to put the two colors on the stick. You can use craft sticks or tongue depressors. After you group the students, collect the sticks so that they are not lost or destroyed.

Number	Color	Color	Number	Color	Color
1	blue	orange	19	yellow	orange
2	yellow	pink	20	green	purple
3	red	purple	21	red	pink
4	green	pink	22	blue	purple
5	yellow	orange	23	green	orange
6	blue	purple	24	yellow	pink
7	green	purple	25	blue	pink
8	red	pink	26	green	purple
9	red	orange	27	red	orange
10	green	orange	28	yellow	orange
11	blue	pink	29	yellow	pink
12	yellow	purple	30	green	purple
13	yellow	purple	31	blue	orange
14	red	orange	32	red	pink
15	green	pink	33	red	purple
16	blue	pink	34	yellow	purple
17	blue	purple	35	bluc	pink
18	red	orange	36	green	orange

Every group of 4 sticks (1–4, 5–8, etc.) has all four colors: green, yellow, blue, and red, one on each stick. If that group of 4 is a team, then the teacher can assign the roles based on the four colors green, yellow, blue, and red. Random groups can be formed by partnering students with the same two colors. Some groups will have 2 students, some 3, and some 4.

To get 4 larger groups, use the colors yellow, green, red, and blue as group identifiers.
To form 3 large groups, use the colors orange, pink, and purple.
To get partners: 1 and 2 are a pair, 3 and 4, 5 and 6, and so on.

Energizing Partners

Establish energizing partners for oral sharing and processing with a partner. Let students choose a classmate with whom they feel they can communicate effectively. For minimal movement, encourage students to chose a partner near where they sit. The partners leave their desks and stand and face each other to share information. Each set of partners decides who is Partner A; the other is Partner B. This helps equalize talking time. The teacher assigns the task and assigns A and B roles and tasks. For example, the teacher says, "Go stand and face your partner. Person A, you share what you remember we discussed from yesterday. Now person B, you share what you remember from yesterday's learning." The established duo can remain partners for a length of time. Some suggested times are a grading period, a semester, or during a particular unit of study. This gives students a time to get out of their seats as well as to discuss the important parts of the learning. Instead of having just one student answer questions, half of the class is engaged in the learning.

Brainstorming Bash

Students form small groups and brainstorm ideas, thoughts, and solutions. After posing the task, give each group member time to answer and process the answer on his or her own. This think time gives each person personal information to share with the group.

Have a recorder in each group write down all the thoughts that are shared. This way the group follows the conversation auditorily and in writing. Consensus may be arrived at with certain tasks assigned to the group through use of a brainstorming list.

Total Class Brainstorming Bash

If the paper is folded with more than one task to complete on the sheet, give the instruction for the first section. Assign a time for completion and a signal for the group to give when finished. Then go to the next set of instructions. This continues throughout the completion of the poster.

Adjustable Assignment Brainstorming Bash

Give specific agenda sheets so that each small group can complete its brainstorming posters with the group's specific tasks.

Community Clusters

Community clusters use small groups to discuss strategies or to share personal thoughts, products, or facts. If the assignment calls for conversations, the teacher can decide the length of the conversation and can ask the students to stand in a "talking circle." Groups work best when they have no more than four students. If the students are sharing products or an artifact, they should form a circle at a table, on the floor, or at a desk cluster.

This group may be used to

♦ Share work findings

♦ Prepare a side of an issue for debate

♦ Process, reflect, and give input into the lesson

♦ Share personal information

Content Talk

Form small groups. Divide the assignment up and let each group be in charge of reading, discussing, or preparing the assigned section with the total group. Assign roles so the responsibility is shared and the groups get the assignment done.

Research Probes

This assignment is given with a chosen or assigned topic to research.

Students often need to come to consensus in their group, choosing what they want to research. Then the desire to find out more about the topic is there. Encourage groups to divide up the assignment among group members.

For example, one student might go to the media center or resource table and look up the information. Another does a Web search, and another interviews and gathers information. Still another student might be the one they give all the found facts to who records and organizes the data.

Experiment, Lab, Center, Station, or Project Groups

Usually, groups of two or three students form the most productive working teams. Sometimes, this kind of group is used because of limited resources and materials; for example, technology equipment, media materials, lab supplies, or manipulatives. Students share information, work together, and produce a product, solve a problem, or learn new methods or processes.

Multiage Grouping

Groups are formed of different ages to learn from each other and work together. For instance, student groups of different age levels can work together with a common goal and learn. This establishes a potential mentoring situation or at least brings unique perspectives from the different age levels that interact with each other. This strategy is useful for reading and computer buddies and problem-solving groups. Several teachers at different grade levels can facilitate the grouping of multiage students. Multiage grouping can also be used to enhance project work and investigation as the diversity of ages brings unique background experiences and knowledge to the tasks. Students learn from role models. Acquisition of language and creative ideas is often shared in these mixed groups.

Remember!

Tap into learning potential! Throughout their lives, students will need to work alone and with others. Learners need experiences in all group types to become effective working citizens in tomorrow's world. Teachers choose the type of group that is appropriate given the task, needs of the students, and targeted standards.

Adjusting, compacting, and grouping are important aspects of the differentiated classroom that meet a diverse audience with curriculum that is more "sized to fit."

Instructional 5 Strategies for Student Success

Just as each learner is unique and one size doesn't fit all, teachers realize that they need a wide repertoire of instructional strategies from which to pick and choose, adjust and modify. Taking a nip and tuck here and there in a garment is a beginning, but alterations are necessary if the garment is to fit comfortably and be wearable.

Although uniqueness is an issue, there are some things we know about how the brain works: It attends to new stimuli, processes information, and stores it in memory.

HOW THE BRAIN WORKS

Let us first examine the process so that we consider it as we think about differentiated instruction. One piece of vital information from brain research is that the brain continues to grow and thrive throughout life from external stimulation in the environment (Kotulak, 1996). The brain is "plastic," which means it changes continually and grows *dendrites* (tree-branch-like connections) between the neurons in response to environmental stimuli and experiences.

Brains change physically in classrooms where students are engaged in meaningful, stimulating experiences. Information is taken into the brain by the senses; this usually is referred to as sensory memory. This is important for survival in the environment. It lasts for approximately three-fourths of a second.

Attention

Of the five senses, visual, tactile, and auditory are the most efficient in capturing attention. There are many environmental factors constantly bombarding our sensory fields to capture our attention. Novelty, color, humor, and hands-on activity all "grab the attention" of the learner. Emotion also plays a large role in increasing attention. Positive or negative emotions may be the "hook" that generates attention or engagement. Strong negative "baggage," such as a bully in the schoolyard or a problem from home, may actually block the attention needed to focus on learning. On the other hand, fun, laughter, play, and a high challenge/low threat environment help focus attention and maintain it.

Memory

Sensory input is either "dumped" out or is passed on to short-term or working memory if the attention is captured.

Once attention takes data from the sensory memory to the short-term or working memory, the data are said to be conscious. The data last in conscious short-term memory up to 20 seconds unless we process them in some way.

We know that the short-term working memory has the capacity for seven bits of information plus or minus two at the mental age of 15 years (Miller, 1956; Pascal-Leon, 1980). This capacity develops over the years, starting at age 5 with two spaces and increasing one space every other year until age 15. One way to deal with more than seven bits is to chunk them into larger pieces that hold more bits.

Rehearsal

Processing in working memory is often called rehearsal. Rehearsal or practice allows us to organize, analyze, make sense of, and remember the information. Rehearsal may be in one of two forms, rote (repeating in the same form) or elaborative (connecting it with known data or embedding it in context).

Elaborative rehearsal facilitates organizing and associating information into networks that are then stored in long-term (unconscious) memory. Rote memory may work for some learning, like multiplication facts that are drilled and memorized and put into automatic memory, but for enduring understanding (Wiggins & McTighe, 1998) to occur, students need more than "drill and kill."

Rote learning does not always have a very long "shelf life" because it has few hooks in the long-term memory. However, the brain is a pattern-seeking device and enjoys making meaning and connections between new ideas and those previously learned. Thus elaborative rehearsal strategies have a greater chance of producing long-term memories.

Rote rehearsal includes

◆ Practice

◆ Recitation

◆ Drill

Elaborative rehearsal includes

◆ Mnemonics[1]

◆ Graphic organizers

◆ Role-plays/simulations

◆ Rhymes/raps

◆ Centers and projects

◆ Using multiple intelligences

◆ Problems/inquiry

◆ Performances

◆ Exhibitions

Context

Context is an important contributor to memory and learning. A field trip to a farm or science center creates strong emotional hooks as well as enriched sensory stimulation. All these aspects will help "Velcro" these experiences and concepts to the mind. *Episodic memory* is a term used to describe contextual or locale learning (O'Keefe & Nadel, 1978). It is processed through the hippocampus, as is declarative memory, which is concerned with the facts (who, what, where, when, and how).

Students often recall information better in the room in which they learned it. The context of the learning brings back vivid experiences of the learning that took place there. Students seem to do better on tests that are taken in the room in which they learned or studied. They also may do better on tests if the teacher who taught them is present in the room.

Emotions

Emotions play a large part not only in garnering attention but also in memory and learning. The amygdala, the brain's emotional sentinel (Goleman, 1995), imprints memory when experiences evoke strong emotions (LeDoux, 1996). Many key events in life and in schools are punctuated by and charged with emotions. For example, we all remember where we were

---

[1]Mnemonics is a way of organizing information to facilitate memory retreival, for example, using H.O.M.E.S. to represent the Great Lakes.

when we heard about the 2001 attack on New York's Twin Towers. This combination of context and emotion creates vivid memories.

Associating Concepts

A way to help students deal with massive amounts of content is to organize information around concepts. For example, students can organize networks of association under concept headings such as Change, Relationships, Persuasion, or Community. These mental concept files can be accessed, and a flood of information will be released as they are opened.

Concepts also help students see the "bigger picture," organize the information, and deepen their understanding. Information is organized in networks of association throughout the neocortex and is unconscious until retrieved back to working memory.

When a "file" of birthdays is opened, for example, all the facts, thoughts, images, memories, and emotions dealing with birthdays comes into conscious awareness. The neural network is searched and asked to recall all it remembers. One idea triggers another. This is why the process of brainstorming is a useful tool for activating prior knowledge. The brain scans the files and one idea brings about another as the connections are revisited.

Recall and Rehearsal

Three things can occur after data have spent time in short-term memory. They may be dumped out (because they have no meaning for the learner or the learner wasn't given any practice), they may be practiced further, or they may be transferred to long-term memory. Once in long-term memory, the data can last forever, but if not used they will become hard to retrieve over time (Pinker, 1998). "Use it or lose it" is true in this case.

Students often need many opportunities to recall and rehearse, many times and in many ways, to deepen their understanding. Doyle and Strauss (1976, p. 25) suggest that we give people too much gum to chew (content) and not enough time to chew it (process). Maybe what we need to retain valuable information is "less gum, more chewing," as suggested by Bob Garnstom, well-known educator and organizational change consultant.

To retrieve information from long-term memory usually takes between 3 and 5 seconds, depending on its quantity and complexity. This is why "wait time" (Rowe, 1988) is so important when asking questions. Because information is stored all over the neocortex in networks of association, it takes time to search those neural networks and bring long-term unconscious memory back to short-term conscious memory.

Figure 5.1. Learning and Remembering New Information: A Complex Process

New information (for example a new flower species) that captures sensory attention (sight, smell, touch, etc.) can be transferred to short-term conscious memory (1). There it can trigger the retrieval of other data (2) already stored in long-term conscious memory about other flower species, in effect opening "flower" files with previous information that have been stored throughout the neocortex (3). By examining and relating the new data to previously learned data, the newer information can be transferred to long-term memory (4), that is, it can be learned and remembered.

Long-term memory is really of two types: declarative and procedural.

Declarative	*Procedural*
The "Facts"	"Autopilot"
Who?	Things one does without thinking
What?	• playing the piano
Where?	• driving a car
Why?	• doing up buttons
When?	• using the computer

Declarative memory is more conscious, whereas procedural memory is unconscious. Procedural memory starts as declarative. For example, when one learns to use a computer, each step is conscious and deliberate. Each step is in declarative memory: turn on switch, wait for screen, insert disk, double click on icon. After many repetitions, the process becomes automatic and can be done unconsciously. These procedures are stored in the cerebellum (little brain). Students require lots of practice to send information and procedures to long-term memory. Practice may occur in a multitude of ways using a variety of Multiple Intelligences and as many modalities as possible to involve opportunities for visual, auditory, and tactile/ kinesthetic learners to develop understanding.

PLANNING INSTRUCTIONAL STRATEGIES

Information about the process of memory is useful for teachers as they plan programs for a diverse group of students so that the students can realize their potential. Teachers may want to ask themselves the following questions as they plan:

- What do I want students to know or be able to do as a result of this learning experience?
- How will we judge success?
- What do they already know and are able to do?
- How can attention be captured and sustained?
- What will the "emotional hook" be for the learners?
- How will new information and skills be acquired?
- How will students practice or rehearse to make meaning and understanding?
- How will they receive ongoing feedback during and after the learning?

FOCUS ACTIVITIES

If teachers are going to capture attention, they need strategies to do so. Focus Activities will

- Help the learner focus and pay attention
- Eliminate distracters
- Open "mental files"
- Provide choices
- Encourage self-directed learning
- Capitalize on "prime time"
- Fill unallocated time—extend or enrich or "sponge" up extra time

Using focus activities at the beginning of class helps students block out distracters, concentrate on activating prior knowledge, and sustain attention. Focus activities can take many forms. One teacher in a math class asked students to do the following with a paper and pencil:

✓ Pick a number from 1 to 9.

✓ Multiply it by 9.

✓ Add the two digits.

✓ Take away 5.

✓ Locate the corresponding letter in the alphabet.

✓ Pick a country that begins with that letter.

✓ Pick an animal that begins with the last letter of the country.

✓ Pick a color that begins with the last letter of your animal. Then the teacher asked the students if they had an orange kangaroo in Denmark.

"Wow," they exclaimed, "How did you know that?" "You figure it out," she challenged them. They eagerly worked in pairs and analyzed the process and discovered that when you multiple any number by 9 the resulting two digits add to 9. Then when you subtract 5 you get 4. The number 4 leads you to D. Under pressure most people choose Denmark as a country. The last letter is K and kangaroo usually comes to mind. The last letter of kangaroo being O leads to the color orange. Then the teacher continued on with reviewing the multiplication table for 9. This teacher knew how to make learning fun, add novelty to the learning, and challenge the students to solve a problem. The brain loves to make sense and seek patterns in information or processes. Other focus activities can take many forms. They may include challenges, questions and problems, or journal entries. Tasks may be offered that require recall and application of previously learned information. For example, students who had read a chapter for homework were asked to sit with a buddy and find as many "feeling" words as they could in the chapter that helped develop the reader's understanding of the character.

Another teacher at the beginning of class had students write down

3 things that they learned in the previous class,

2 ideas that connected for them, and

1 question they had for today.

Often, teachers use a K-W-L chart (Ogle, 1986). The K stands for what students already know about the topic. The W stands for what the students want to know. The L is used at the end of the lesson or unit of study to enable students to reflect on their learning and identify the information and processes learned. Sometimes, teachers offer choices to students in order to capitalize on their interests and give them options. These techniques are also forms of pre-assessment that help the teacher and students set goals and design and select learning tasks appropriate to individuals or groups of learner.

The following example is a set of focus tasks that a teacher offered to students to allow them to make a choice:

> From the chapter that you read last night, choose one of the following tasks and work alone or with a partner to complete it:
>
> ✓ Draw a comic strip to show the events in the chapter.
>
> ✓ In your journal, chronicle the events in the chapter.
>
> ✓ Describe the setting and how it related to the events in the chapter.
>
> ✓ If you were a newscaster, what would your progress report be?
>
> ✓ Rewrite a passage of the chapter in your own words. Use synonyms to replace some of the author's words.

SPONGE ACTIVITIES

Throughout the day there may be times when students finish work early. The teacher can offer other tasks to "sponge" up the extra time without wasting instructional time. Tasks may also be provided for students to use as sponge activities when extra time is available. These tasks are also useful when the teacher is working with one group and students in other groups finish what they were doing. These sponge activities help students become more self-directed learners. Sometimes, the students will focus on a personal quest or project that they are pursuing or some standard or skill that they are trying to master. Broader or more general tasks may be offered, such as the following:

♦ Develop a crossword puzzle on the computer to review the topic.

♦ Use the computer to develop a word web on this concept or topic.

♦ Revise your agenda for the week.

♦ Work on your culminating task for the unit.

♦ Use a word web to organize the ideas in this unit.

♦ Examine the items in your portfolio and make some decisions regarding the pieces you have included. Should some be deleted or replaced at this point?

These more generic tasks may be posted for the week for all to refer to when they have some time to "sponge" up productively.

GRAPHIC ORGANIZERS

What Are They?

Graphic organizers are useful thinking tools that allow students to organize information and allow students see their thinking. They are visual/spatial, logical/mathematical tools that appeal to many learners for managing and organizing information. Graphic organizers give visual representations of facts/concepts and also they show the relationship between and among new facts and previous information. They are also used to plot processes and procedures. Graphic organizers can be utilized at many points in the lesson.

Why Use Them?

The difference between good and poor learners is not the sheer quantity of what the good learner learns, but rather the good learner's ability to organize and use information (Frank Smith, 1986).

Graphic organizers can be used

♦ For brainstorming at the beginning of a lesson or unit to find out what students already know

♦ With reading assignments or when watching a video so that students can organize and capture information. The teacher may provide one, or students can design their own using the criteria given by the teacher, such as Who? What? Where? and Why?

♦ To help chronicle a sequence of events or a process

♦ To relate new information to previously learned information

♦ To check for understanding

♦ For note taking and summarizing

♦ For the culminating assessment

How Do We Use Them?

As with any tool, students need to be taught how to use the organizer and be given opportunities for practice with a full range of content and situations. Teachers model how the organizer can be used with content that is not too complicated. That way students learn the process of using the organizer and can then use it with any content. Over time, students become familiar with the process of using a variety of graphic organizers. They will become adept at choosing appropriate organizers to fit the situation. Many students begin to design and create their own organizers to fit their needs. Using visual representations often appeals to the intrapersonal learner, who appreciates opportunities for processing and reflecting on new information independently. Organizers can be used independently, with a partner, or in a small group.

Instructional strategies that increase student achievement (Marzano et al., 2000) are comparing, contrasting, classifying, and using metaphors. Students who spend time looking at the similarities and differences between two topics and perhaps plot these on a graphic organizer deepen their understanding and ability to use the knowledge. The often-used Venn diagram (Figure 5.2) identifies what is similar and what is different between two topics. A quick way to teach students to use the Venn is to have them compare themselves with a classmate as to personal characteristics, likes and dislikes, hobbies or sports, pets, and so on. They can brainstorm these characteristics individually and then plot them on the Venn with their partner, placing similarities in the overlapping center and the differences on each side.

A comparison matrix (Figure 5.3) is another way to compare several items based on identified criteria. For example, when comparing states, the following could be listed in the left column: New York, Arizona, California, and Louisiana. Across the top, the following criteria could be considered: climate, population, geography, and size. This information, once plotted, can be transferred to a Venn diagram to identify the similarities and differences between two of the states.

Other forms of comparing and contrasting can be used. In Figure 5.4, any two things, ideas, concepts, or procedures may be scrutinized. At the top, in the first two frames, the two things being analyzed are put in place. In the two large boxes underneath, all their attributes are listed. Then all their similarities are selected and placed in the large frame underneath the Similarities heading. Finally, the ways in which the concepts differ are placed in the appropriate frames. Use the numbers so that the items in each box that differ correspond to one another. Students can compare forms of art, continents, scientific procedures, politicians, or historical events or any two pieces of content in any subject area.

Figure 5.2. Venn Diagram Used to Identify an Area of Overlap Between Two Topics

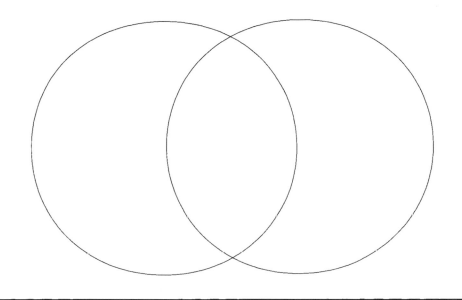

Figure 5.3. Cross-Classification Compare and Contrast Matrix

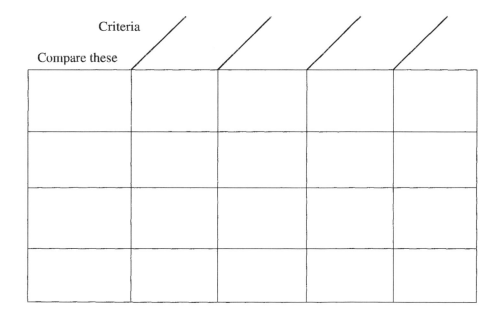

Figure 5.4. Comparing 2 Things Flow Chart

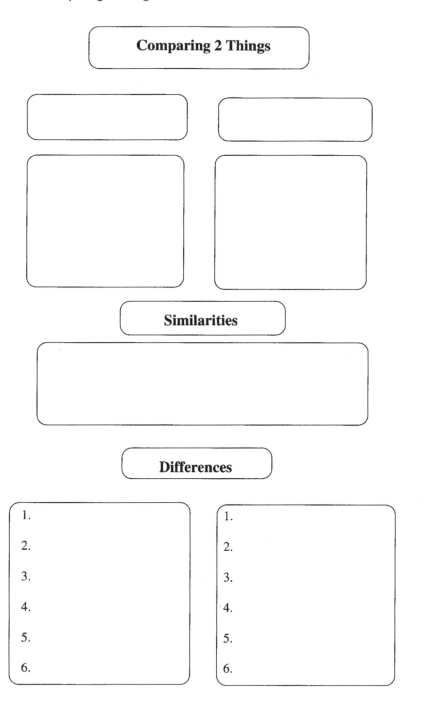

The web is an organizer that can be used for organizing and classifying. It enables students to focus on a concept, theme, or topic; identify the secondary categories related to the big idea; and then add all the significant dimensions related to those secondary categories. In Figure 5.5, the big idea is World War II; the secondary categories are the Axis, the Allies, Causes, Differences, Theatres of War, the Blitzkrieg, and Pivotal Events.

Figure 5.5.   Example of a Word Web Used to Organize and Classify Primary and Secondary Concepts Related to World War II

A word web can be used to assess how well students have organized data. It also indicates that they have grasped the major concepts, and made connections between them. It is also a useful tool to organize thinking in the prewriting stage.

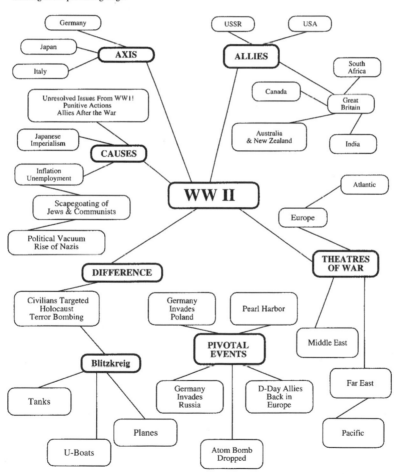

SOURCE: Used with permission from Terence Parry.

The quality of thinking, classifying, and deep understanding that it takes to create an intricate word web is a form of elaborative thinking and processing.

The following are suggested ways to use the Graphic organizers shown in Figure 5.6:

1. Fact Frame: Write fact in center box. Write supporting details in outer box

2. Roll It: Write topic in the tire section. Write four key points in the spokes.

3. Inside Out: Write an important event, object, character, or place in the center. Write its attributes in the outer oval.

4. Angle Antics: Put a cause in each big triangle. Write the effects on each side of the cause.

5. Star Connections: Place the topic in the middle. Add a key fact in each star point.

6. Drumming Up Details: Write a prediction on the top of the drum. State the outcomes or learned facts on the side of the drum.

Figure 5.6. Graphic Organizer Framework

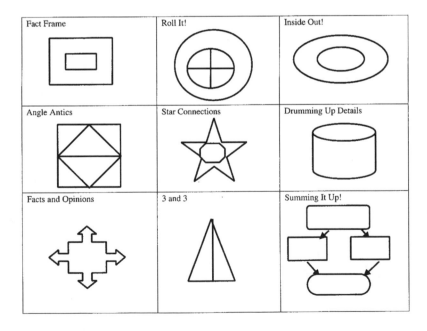

7. Fact and Opinions: Write the fact in the center. List an opinion by each arrow.

8. 3 and 3: Write an important topic vocabulary noun in each of the large triangles. Write the meaning, a sentence, and draw a picture on the sidelines.

9. Summing It Up!: In the top rectangle, write the fact. In the next two boxes, write two supporting details. Then write the summary or conclusion in the bottom figure.

METAPHORS

Using metaphors and analogies is another way to show similarities and differences and to connect new information to more familiar objects or concepts. In Chapter 2, "Knowing the Learner," we used the objects beach ball, microscope, clipboard, and puppy to help clarify and understand the characteristics of the four styles of learning. By thinking of these four objects, one can easily recall the attributes of each the objects and in turn relate those characteristics to the four learning styles to understand them better.

Students can also relate new information by connecting it to something with which they are familiar. They may be able to understand the Renaissance if we ask them to explain how the Renaissance is like a video game, or understand the government if we ask them how the government is like an orchestra. When using two seemingly unrelated ideas or topics we are causing students to examine comparisons and look at the similarities and differences between the two.

Having students stretch their thinking through metaphorical connections increases the likelihood of broadening their understanding of a concept or topic and remembering it in the future.

COOPERATIVE GROUP LEARNING

Cooperative group learning is one of the most researched instructional strategies in education today. We have gained valuable insight over the years from revered educators such as Aronson (1978), Bellanca and Fogarty (1991), Bennett, Bennett-Rolheiser, and Stevhan (1991), Cantelon (1991a, 1991b), Clarke, Wideman, and Eadie (1990) Johnson, Johnson, and Holubec (1998), and Kagan (1992). Working in cooperative groups, students learn valuable social skills, use higher-order thinking, and rehearse and practice new concepts, processes, and information. Cooperative group learning does not happen successfully unless it is well orchestrated and certain considerations prevail. These considerations increase the chances that the groups will work well together and achieve targeted standards (Johnson et al., 1998).

The acronym TASK (Robbins, Gregory, & Herndon, 2000) can be used to remember these aspects of cooperative group learning:

T   Thinking is built into the process

A   Accountability is essential. Goal achievement: both individual and group

S   Social skills for team success

K   Keeping everyone on TASK: Roles, tasks, resources, novelty, simulations, and clear expectations

Thinking Skills Are Built Into the Process

Cooperative group learning is ideal for embedding a variety of other instructional strategies that make a difference in student learning. Graphic organizers, thinking skills, and metaphors are easily used in cooperative group work to facilitate rehearsal and practice. Groups can be given tasks that are differentiated and adjusted to levels of the thinking taxonomy (see Figures 1.1 and 1.2 in Chapter 1). This will challenge groups at a variety of levels.

Cubing is a strategy that works well in cooperative groups. Opportunities to explore content by using some or all of the Multiple Intelligences are possible. Students see many sides of a topic when using multiple intelligence as a lens.

Accountability Is Essential

Students who work together in cooperative groups generally produce a group product or a project that is graded. Each student needs to be accountable for his or her personal contributions to the group and also for personal acquisition of knowledge and skills as a result of the group process. Teachers often use checklists or journal entries to collect data on the contributions and learning of individuals in the group. If teachers need to know what students know and have learned in the group session, individual tests, quizzes, demonstrations, exhibitions, and conferences will help clarify the understanding and competencies of each of the students. Cooperative group learning is a powerful strategy for learning, but we can't assume that everyone will know and understands the content and develop the skills just by being in a group.

Assessment may be multifaceted and include

♦ An individual grade for the piece of work completed or the part of the presentation given

♦ A group grade for the final product or presentation

♦ A test or quiz on the content

♦ A mark for group participation

Using cooperative groups for the learning process and assessing students individually is a good way to begin. As students become accustomed to working in groups and really pull together, teachers can move toward more group grading.

Social Skills for Team Success

Even though teachers work to build climate and trust in the classroom, they may also need to teach social skills. Cooperative group learning not only helps students learn content and competencies but also helps them develop their emotional intelligence in the five domains (Goldman, 1995):

♦ Self-awareness: through reflection

♦ Self-motivation: developing persistence and a positive work ethic

♦ Managing emotions: learning strategies for conflict resolution and consensus building

♦ Empathy: listening, reflecting feelings, behaving in a supportive manner

♦ Social skills: opportunities to identify practice and reflect on social skills

Students have different needs in these areas, and teachers will observe where those needs are as they monitor groups and recognize the strengths and weaknesses of their students.

Basic social skills that students need include

♦ Using appropriate language

♦ Speaking politely and quietly

♦ Encouraging others

◆ Listening to others

◆ Asking for help

Some social skills that students need to function well in a group include

◆ Disagreeing in an agreeable way

◆ Accepting different opinions

◆ Following procedures

◆ Checking for accuracy and understanding

◆ Dealing with conflict

Students need to know what a social skill "looks like, sounds like and feels like" (Hill & Hancock, 1993) through conscious identification of the skill, modeling, practice, and feedback.

Teachers often post charts for reference that describe acceptable behavior in the classroom. Students need to contribute to the charts using their own language and terms. This increases clarity and ownership of the behavior and the probability that it will be practiced. Figure 5.7 is an example of a chart that describes "listening to others." It was developed by a teacher and students during a conversation about the importance of listening to other people in a group.

Students then need to practice this skill with their group and reflect on its use.

Individuals learn differently as a result of their experience and need a chance to contemplate their learning and their participation. Because students sometimes don't have the ability for reflection without guidelines, an organizer may be provided. Figure 5.8 is an example of student reflection after a group effort.

Figure 5.7. Social Skill: Listening to Others

Looks like	Sounds like	Feels like
Looking at the person	Tell me more . . .	I've been heard
Nodding and smiling	Mmm . . .	My ideas are valued

Figure 5.8.   Reflection on Group Work

Date: _____

Name: _____

In my math class today we were involved in a cooperative
learning activity.
This is a summary of what my group did.

My role was . . .

_____

_____

My behavior in that role was . . .

_____

_____

I helped achieve the group goal by . . .

_____

_____

I could have . . .

_____

_____

One thing I need to work on is . . .

_____

_____

Keeping Students on Task

Students in cooperative groups usually are assigned roles that increase the chances that they will work interdependently (Johnson et al., 1988). Roles can be assigned to keep the group functioning well, such as encourager, clarifier, summarizer, or questioner. Other roles may include those that facilitate the task, such as recorder, reader, researcher, drawer, materials manager, or reporter. This encourages students to take responsibility and ownership for the task by assuming a particular role.

Some teachers may want to set up a scenario more like the real world and assign some of the following roles to the students in a cooperative group (from Kathy & Rob Bocchino, Heart of Change Consultants).

Production Manager: The production manager is responsible for the project. You will oversee and ensure that the other managers are working appropriately. You will manage the process, keep track of progress, and will be the only person in the group who communicates with the CEO (teacher) when the group needs clarification or direction.

Information Manager: Your job is to ensure the accuracy and quality of the product. Your listening skills are valuable assets and help you make sure you clarify what the client is asking for. You will make sure all group members understand the client's/CEO's expectations. You must adhere to any written directions.

Resource Manager: Your job is to gather and manage the materials necessary to complete the group project. Make sure all group papers and materials are properly stored away at the end of the period. If other objects, props, or materials are necessary, arrange to acquire them and make sure they are available when needed.

Personnel Manager: Your job is to manage the people on the team and build morale throughout the production. Encourage other team members, manage conflicts, and facilitate problem solving when necessary. Monitor for effort and productivity. Communicate any concerns to the production manager

Technology Manager: Your job is to assist group members with all technical aspects of the production. You will assist members with their computer skills when using the Internet for research, with spreadsheets and databases, word processing, presentation techniques, and troubleshooting.

Time Manager: Your job is to know when all deadlines are and remind others in the production team of those deadlines. You will keep a log of the steps and the progress. Communicate with the production manager concerning time lines and concerns. Communicate with the production manager concerning a particular team member who is not meeting time requirements. If more time is needed, ask the production manager to negotiate for more time.

Teachers also can increase the interdependence in the groups

♦ By creating a sequence to the process: Each group member has a role and particular step to perform in the task

♦ By providing limited resources (tools, texts, materials) that must be shared to complete the activity

♦ By providing novelty and engaging scenarios or simulations in which students take on a persona such as an investigator, researcher, or land developer. This creates a role that would be found in the real world and often adds authenticity to the activity.

Using Cooperative Group Learning

There are many times when students work in cooperative groups of two, three, or four. In fact, working in pairs is a great way to start to build alliances in the classroom by getting to work with many students to get to know them. It is also hard to get left out of a pair (Johnson et al., 1988). Partner work gives students a chance to practice social skills in a controlled environment with only one other personality at a time. It also builds community as students get to know one another one-on-one.

Whenever cooperative group learning is used as a vehicle for student learning, teachers need to ask the following questions to clarify the intention and process for the learning:

♦ What is it that students need to accomplish, and how will I communicate that? (Written task cards or charted directions should be clearly outlined for students so that expectations are clear and visible to all)

♦ What will the size of the group be, considering the task?

♦ How will I group students and why? (Randomly, by ability, by background knowledge, heterogeneous but structured; see Figures 4.9, "Wagon Wheel Teams," and 4.10, "Stick Picks")

◆ What social skill will they practice and reflect on? (Social skill should be relevant to the task)

◆ How will they learn about the social skill?

◆ How will they monitor its use?

◆ What are the timelines and guidelines for the task?

◆ What assessment will be used for the academic task? (Presentation, product, report, performance, exhibition, test, quiz, etc.)

◆ What roles or tasks will group members be assigned to ensure interdependence and active participation?

One way to increase interdependence is by using a jigsaw method.

JIGSAW

Jigsaw (Aronson, 1978; Slavin, 1994; see Figure 5.9) is a very effective strategy, but not one that would be used with students until they have the social skills to deal with several members in a group as well as the skills to work independently. It is a powerful strategy for covering more material in less time. It enhances learning and increases retention. Students begin in a base group of three or four and are given letters or number or names that will help them form expert groups. In the expert group, students are to access information or learn new material or skills that they will in turn teach

Figure 5.9. Jigsaw Strategy: Used to Enhance Interdependence With More Advanced Learners

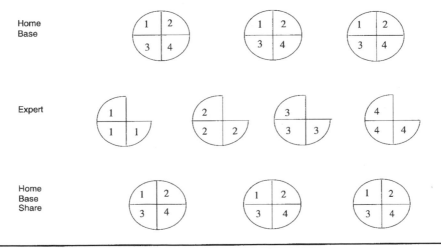

to their base group. When they return to the base group, they teach their group members what they have learned.

Individual accountability is built into the process by having each member hand in a report, a test, or quiz on the material learned or by calling on students randomly to report for their group.

The Jigsaw method facilitates the sharing of responsibility for learning. It helps focus energy in a task and provides structure and process for the learning. It has inter/intrapersonal components that also allow students to process information and move and interact with a variety of class members to gain a greater perspective on the knowledge or skills that are targeted for learning. If offers many chances for elaborative rehearsal and use of higher-order thinking through dialogue.

Jigsaws can be differentiated for students by giving them different materials and content to match different levels of readiness. Products, projects, or other authentic tasks and assessment that are expected from the group, based on their preferences and multiple intelligences, offer another way to differentiate.

The following example is a way of building in all the aspects of TASK.

The Character Sketch (Figure 5.10) is an organizer that can be used by a cooperative group of four people when reading a story or novel. Groups A and B would focus on the same character (perhaps the main character). Groups C and D would identify a different character, and so on. The base group (persons 1, 2, 3, & 4) would cut the organizer on the broken line and distribute the four sections. Each person in Group A would meet with the same number partner from group B (i.e., 1 with 1, 2 with 2, 3 with 3, and 4 with 4). They would discuss an aspect of the character depending on the section of the organizer that they have. For example, two students may have the quadrant that says "Looks like." They would find evidence in the story of what the character looks like and then write their conclusions in that segment of the quadrant. As they work together, the social skill they use would be to clarify information and listen to others' ideas. Each group of partners would meet and complete their section of the organizer: Looks like, Seems like, Does, and Sounds like. Then the base groups would reconstitute and review all the evidence and conclusions that they made. From this information, the group would write a complete character sketch based on all the attributes collected.

The organizer can be reproduced on large chart paper to increase the space for collected information and to allow all participants to see the information. Each group member would have an organizer to collect data personally from other expert team members.

This activity is called a jigsaw. There is interdependence built in through shared resources and tasks. The students practice social skills as they work. They access information and use evidence to support their thinking, both worthy standards in any classroom.

Figure 5.10. Character Sketch: Used as an Organizer by Four Students When Reading a Story or Novel.

Character:

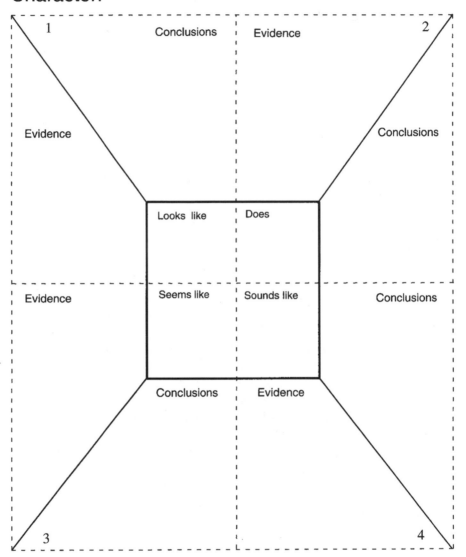

This organizer can also be modified and used to divide tasks in other subject areas in a jigsaw process as well. Students could begin in a base group and examine four aspects of a country, such as food, peoples, geography, and origins (or in Biology they could focus on body systems such as respiratory, digestive, nervous, and circulatory) in their expert groups and bring that information back to their base group.

ROLE-PLAYING

What Is It?

Role-play is when students take on the role of a character, perhaps from a story, play, or novel, a historical or political figure, or someone depicting a particular scenario that deals with a concern or issue such as conflict resolution.

Why Do We Do It?

Role-playing allows students to process knowledge and demonstrate skills in an emotionally laden context. It is a form of elaborative rehearsal that causes students to interact with content and concepts and, ideally, create an episodic memory. It affords students the opportunity to examine and organize information, deal with issues, and create or re-create situations that have meaning. The roles students take on allow them to become immersed in situations. They become that person or character and take on that persona. As they play that role, their emotions are involved and the emotional brain punctuates the moment. Role-play allows students to be involved at their level. Many students have strong verbal and interpersonal skills, and this technique allows them to use those skills.

How Do We Do It?

Allow students the opportunity to be involved when they are comfortable. Encourage volunteers who are willing to participate. Teachers find that they must work within the comfort zones of students, as those who are more intrapersonal do not always embrace this technique because they may not be as gregarious as other students. Initially, teachers may have students engage in improvisation. As teachers begin to introduce this technique to students, they may want to use mime initially or provide a script. After several tries at role-playing, students may begin to write scripts for themselves. Props and scenery may be included if needed or available.

All students will need to identify appropriate audience interaction and behavior and monitor that behavior in role-play situations. Feedback to participants should be positive and constructive. Reflection and emotional reactions should be processed after each attempt at role play. Role-plays place information and key concepts in a contextual learning situation and increase the chances for understanding and retention.

Teachers who use a variety of instructional strategies add novelty, choice, and individuality to the learning. These strategies allow diverse learners to find a size that fits and suits and to engage in practice and rehearsal to deepen understanding through as many learning styles and multiple intelligences as they can.

There are numerous instructional strategies, and we continue to learn and add to our expertise, like adding clothes to our wardrobe. However, as teachers build and increase their repertoire they will see how they can adjust the learning for the group of learners and how different strategies appeal to different learners.

One size doesn't fit all and, happily, one size doesn't have to.

Curriculum 6
Approaches for
Differentiated
Classrooms

Individual items of clothing are put together to form a wardrobe. Wardrobes evolve and build over time as we add and discard articles. A variety of instructional tools develop, and when used strategically are powerful in a differentiated classroom. They can be built into various curriculum approaches. Curriculum can be delivered in many ways so it will appeal to individual learners and their needs for novelty, engaging activities, and quests for meaning. In this chapter, we explore centers, projects, problem-based learning, inquiry, and contracts.

One way to organize curriculum is to use centers or stations.

CENTERS

What Are They?

A center is a collection of material, designed purposely, with a goal in mind.

Students work with center materials to develop, discover, create, and learn a task at their own pace. Students are responsible for their learning during center time. There is always an established purpose for each center.

The hands-on experiences in centers provide opportunities for learners to

♦ Remediate, enhance, or extend knowledge on a skill, concept, standard, or topic

♦ Pursue interests and explore the world of knowledge

♦ Work at the level of need and be challenged

♦ Be creative and critical problem solvers

♦ Make choices, establish their own pace, and build persistence

♦ Manipulate a variety of different types of materials

♦ Facilitate complex thinking and dendritic growth

Centers are an ideal design for adjustable assignments.
Centers can be set up in different ways:

1. A variety of centers on a topic or theme in a particular subject area with different levels of difficulty

2. Interest centers for further investigation of a topic

3. Free inventing centers for experimenting, discovering, and inventing

4. Computer centers with multimedia resources for supplemental or remedial use

5. Resource centers with a wide variety of reading materials

6. Art media table to create artifacts that represent learning and creativity

7. Role-playing centers to demonstrate characters and sequence of events

8. Manipulatives centers for hands-on learning

9. Skills centers for adjustable assignments

10. Writing centers with a variety of writing tools and various types and sizes of paper

11. Challenge centers for problem solving

12. Listening centers with music or readings from both fictional and factual content

13. Multiple intelligences centers that provide students with choices related to the topic

A structured center has specific tasks assigned and an agenda developed by the teacher. During center time, students work with skills or concepts, approaching them through a variety of experiences. Multilevel tasks are often designed for a certain skill or objective for this type of center. During center time, students work at their level of need, and at their own pace while being challenged with complex, hands-on learning (see also Chapman & Freeman, 1996).

An exploratory center has materials provided and allows the student to decide what to do with those materials. For example, a reading nook is available with a wide variety of different types of reading materials. The student decides which material to read and how long to read. A student settles down to read a selection because of a high interest in the topic and an appropriate reading level (see also Chapman & Freeman, 1996).

Establishing centers facilitates many diverse opportunities for learning to take place. The teacher can consciously adjust activities for the centers in the planning process and assign appropriate learners to the various centers. Centers are places where the work can be made to fit the learner's needs, ranging from basic learning, to remediation, to enrichment. They set up opportunities for understanding a skill or a concept through a variety of experiences. By having a variety of materials and tasks at one station, students become more responsible for their learning. They make their own choices and set individualized goals. There is an intrinsic reward for self-achievement. Centers provide opportunities to pursue individual interests and talents with greater immersion in the topic.

How Do We Use Them?

Choice Centers

Secondary history teacher Diane Huggler (Corning, NY) set up Ancient Civilization Learning Centers that included the students' choice of China, Japan, Africa, the Middle East, Southwest Asia, and the Pacific.

The Goal

Your group's task is to discover as much about your civilization as you can from a variety of sources and present the information to the class.

The Procedure

- Each group has a set of color-coded folders that explain criteria for this task and help you discover information about your ancient people.

- Each person in the group will have a certain role within the group to make sure that it functions smoothly and completes its task successfully.

- Class time is to be used to complete the folder activities. Record your progress in the group log/journal.

The Presentation

- You will become the experts on your civilization, and you have the opportunity to share your knowledge with your classmates.

◆ Your group needs to prepare a PowerPoint presentation, with *each* group member being responsible for at least two slides.

◆ You may also use other teaching tools, such as the overhead projector, the chalkboard, maps, pictures, and so on, to tap the Multiple Intelligences.

◆ Your presentation needs to be at least 15 minutes long, and you need to be prepared to answer classmates' questions.

The Grade

◆ You will be assessed in three areas using a rubric that identifies how well you performed in the following categories:

1. Content

2. Presentation

3. Group skills

4. A multiple-choice test that will be given at the end of the unit and that will cover all the groups' presentations

Another scenario is the creation of Math Rotation Centers. Students work in each center to complete all tasks. They sign into centers the day before and keep track on their agenda.

Center 1

Stock Update: Students are involved in a simulation of creating their own stock portfolios, where they buy and sell stocks, and keep track of the profit or loss.

Students are directed to complete the first update sheet in their stock folder, identifying profit or loss. They use information online or in the newspapers provided.

Center 2

Folder Check: Examine and organize your math portfolio. Your portfolio should include notes, mental math papers, reflections, and mind maps of solutions, followed by all graded papers with corrections. Be sure your reflection is attached. When you finish your folder, you may move on to . . . the "BIG ONE" and Fraction Card Game: This center involves playing games with others in your color group. The key concept is identifying equivalent fractions. Games may be played only after all players have completed their folder check.

Center 3

Changing Fractions to Decimals: This center uses Versa Tiles to self-correct activities. These tasks involve a basic understanding of finding equivalent fractions and decimals as well as an introduction to ratios.

Center 4

Chocolate Delight: At this center you take an $8\frac{1}{2}'' \times 11''$ sheet of paper and fold it in half as per the instructions. After renaming the equivalent fractions, please write the explanation on the back of half the paper. Then proceed to the self-correcting worksheets using a dry-erase marker. Please erase all answers when finished.

Thematic Centers: Experiments

The theme of these centers, adapted from versions used by the Halton Board of Education (Halton, Ontario), was Eggs. The centers consisted of scientific experiments that were part of an integrated unit called "Great Eggspectations." The examples in Figures 6.1 and 6.2 show the planning for two of the centers, paying attention to

♦ Standards and content

♦ Who will be working in the center

♦ Activities

♦ Materials needed

♦ Location

♦ Assessment

♦ Teacher reflections

Figure 6.3 has templates that may be used to plan centers.

Management Techniques

Establish clearly defined, effective workspaces for centers. They might be a desktop, a carpet square, a lab station, a table, or a corner of the room. They are spaces for working with a particular set of materials related to particular tasks.

When setting up the centers be sure to label the materials. For instance, if certain pieces go with one task, color code or put a symbol on them to coordinate them as a set to enable quick identification. Also give them a "home" so they can be found and returned to the same location. This way the materials are organized and labeled properly for easy access. Students need to assist in the distribution and cleaning up of materials. Design a system that is easy and efficient. Consider the uniqueness of the situation

(text continues on page 113)

Figure 6.1. Center Example: The Magic Egg

Center: The Magic Egg

Standards: Recognize changes in matter

Content: To demonstrate the semipermeability of a cell membrane. The shell is affected by vinegar and carbon dioxide forms. The membrane will turn rubbery. The egg will swell because the contents of the egg cannot pass through the tiny holes in the membrane. The water in the vinegar passes through the membrane into the egg and causes it to swell.

Who: Group of 4, heterogeneous group

Activities	Materials
Small group: 1. Measure around the center of the egg and record. 2. Describe the egg. 3. Place the egg in the jar. Do not break the shell. 4. Cover the egg with vinegar. 5. Close the lid. 6. Look at it right away and then look at it at different times for the next 3 days. 7. Remove the egg after 3 days and measure once again around its middle. 8. Compare what the egg looks like now and before it was in the vinegar.	• 1 raw egg • 1 jar with a lid (the egg must fit in the jar) • Clear vinegar • Measuring tape that is flexible **Location** Table in corner of room by the window. Roles for group members: 1. Recorder 2. Materials handler 3. Reader and reporter
Assessment	**Teacher Reflections**
Predictions. Group booklet will be produced containing recordings of the experiments. Cooperative skills reflection.	

Figure 6.2. Center Example: Bottled Egg

Center: Bottled Eggs

Standards: To develop scientific principles of experimentation. To develop the skills of hypothesis, inference and prediction, problem solving and decision making.

Objectives: To determine a way in which one can fit a hard-boiled egg through a small necked bottle without breaking it.

Who: Group of 4, heterogeneous group

Activities	Materials
Teacher information: Hot water creates and leaves steam in the bottle and that forces out some air. When the steam changes to droplets of water, it doesn't need as much space. So the air pressure is reduced and the pressure of the air outside the bottle forces the egg into the bottle. Directions for group: 1. Pour boiling water into the bottle. 2. Shake it around and then pour it out. 3. Place the egg over the mouth of the bottle. 4. Record your observations. 5. To remove the egg, turn the bottle upside down, and place your mouth over the opening and blow into it for about half a minute.	• A hard-boiled egg, peeled • A small-necked jar (slightly smaller than the egg) • Boiling water **Location** Small group by table near the sink. Roles for group members: • Recorder, reporter • Materials manager • Encourager (reader)

Assessment	Teacher Reflections
Were the students successful in placing the egg in and out of the bottle? Group log and findings Group reflection	

Figure 6.3. Center Planning Templates

Center:	
Standards:_____	
Content:_____	
_____	
_____	
Who : _____	

Activities	Materials
	Location
Assessment	**Teacher Reflections**

and plan accordingly. It is better to prethink management strategies than to have things go "off the rails" and thus waste valuable learning time while you rethink logistics.

Establish and teach rules so that all participants have a common understanding. Many times the expectations for the regular classroom will also cover center work.

For example, "Work quietly and respect others" is as relevant in centers as anywhere in the classroom.

Establish a common signal to get students' attention so all the students know what the signal is and what to do when they hear it. This is valuable when directions need to be given to a large group or when it is time to clean up.

Sometimes, students finish their work at a center before the time for center work is finished. That's when focus or sponge activities come into play. There should always be something meaningful and productive to do next. Often, it can be a reflection or journal or log entry or another form of student self-assessment.

At times, the teacher is stationed in a center. Students rotate and come to the teacher's table to work. This works well when the teacher needs to give special attention to a particular group. The students at the other centers learn to self-monitor and become self-directed learners.

When centers have been set up based on interests or when students use them for sponge activities, they can eventually lose their appeal. At this point, the teacher should introduce a new interest center based on his or her observations and assessment of students' needs and preference.

Students are often allowed to go to a new center of interest if time permits. Teacher monitoring and conferencing about quality work will mediate the decision to move on to a new center.

How Do We Assess?

One way to discover the thinking processes that students use when approaching tasks or problems is assessing center time. When asked the appropriate questions, students make their thinking known to the teacher. Assessment shows if or where students have difficulties and which parts they understand and which need clarification. Proper assistance and follow-up can then be given to keep the students learning at their own rates toward the targeted standards.

Assessment during center time is essential. Students and teachers continue to dialogue, to give and receive feedback. Teachers who ask the right questions during this time can learn so much about their students. When open-ended questions are asked, students tell their thinking and explain their process. Expressing orally how they solved that particular problem or accomplished a task lets students become more metacognitive and reflective about their tasks. Using anecdotal note taking or an observation checklist along with effective questions, teachers learn where the students are in their learning and often where they need to go next. Assessment should inform practice and tell us how students are progressing and what adjustments should be made to a program.

Both the students and the teacher should pay attention to assessment data to inform the next steps.

Teacher Assessment Strategies

Teachers move in and out the centers to interact with the learners and monitor their progress. Ongoing conferencing keeps learners on task and gives teachers the data necessary to adjust or change any activities that are not challenging enough or perhaps are too challenging. Ongoing modification is often necessary to adjust tasks when there is a need to do so.

Assessment Tools

Anecdotal Finding. Teachers often record anecdotal findings of observations for record-keeping purposes.

Some teachers refer to this as "clipboard cruising" (see Figure 6.4). The data collection sheet may look something like the one in Figure 6.4, with columns for note taking.

Checklists. Use a checklist to assess the behaviors being observed. Teachers observing center time design the most effective checklists because they are familiar with the information and its location on the list. It should take longer to develop the checklist than to score it. The teacher who will be using it designs the most effective checklist; each item fits a particular situation. Also if the person who made the checklist is the one scoring it that person is familiar with the data and it is easy to use.

Center time checklists (Figure 6.5) should address the targeted needs of the group. One list could address social skills, another, time cognitive skills, and yet another, both. Figure 6.5 offers some sample observable behaviors to include in a checklist.

Effective Questioning Techniques

Open-ended Questions and Statements. Have students demonstrate what they know by asking appropriate questions. The right questions get students to convey their thinking processes, which are unique to how each student approaches a task or problem at a particular time. This evidence shows where there are weaknesses and strengths, misunderstandings or clarity.

Some examples of effective questions are

♦ Tell me what you are doing.

♦ How did you do that?

♦ Tell me step by step how you made that.

Student Self-Assessment

Students can use log and journal entries for self-assessment. Some suggestions for logs or journals include

a. Today I want to tell you _____

Choose one of the following that you would like to share:

♦ What I am doing

♦ Why I am doing it

♦ Why it is important

♦ How I can use it

♦ Why I chose to do this

♦ What I need next

Figure 6.4.   Clipboard Cruising for Data Collection

Clipboard Cruising

Name	Date	Time	Center or Task	Observed behavior

Figure 6.5. Center Checklists: Used to Address Targeted Needs of the Group

Center Checklist

Name _____ Center _____ Unit of Study_____
Type of assignment _____Assigned ____ Student Choice_____
Teacher Date _____ Signature _____
Peer   Date _____Signature _____
Self   Date _____Signature _____

Work Habits	*Not Yet*	*Sometimes*	*Most of the time*
Stays on task			
Gets work done on time			
Uses materials appropriately			
Completes tasks			
Follows rules at the center			
Uses time wisely			
Social skills			
Shares materials			
Listens to others			
Helps others			
Respects self and others			
Shows patience			
Group work			
Takes turns			
Shares materials and ideas			
Participates appropriately			
Focuses on one person talking			
Communicates appropriately			
Works well with others			
Helps others			

COMMENTS:

b. Four Thoughts Feedback_____

- ♦ The part I like best is _____
- ♦ The part I am not clear about is _____
- ♦ Someone needs to tell me more about _____
- ♦ Next time I need to _____

c. Today I will receive the _____award.
Make an award certificate or ribbon.

Centers themselves can be assessed by students after they have worked in them. Cards may be placed at the centers for students to give their feedback to the teacher (Figure 6.6). You may want to include some or all of the information in the figure.

Journal entries are also useful after center work. Here are a few suggestions for journal stems that help students reflect on their work:

- ♦ The best thing about this center time was _____
- ♦ The worst thing about this center time was _____
- ♦ Next time I _____
- ♦ I learned _____
- ♦ This is what I did, step by step: _____

Figure 6.6. Sample Feedback Card for Students to Assess Centers After They Have Worked in Them

Name_____Center: _____Date: _____

At this center I learned _____

_____

_____

Centers that I worked in today were
1. _____
2. _____

While I was there I _____

How would you rate your learning?   1   2   3   4   5   Wow

Center time can be some of the most productive time in the classroom. When the centers are set up with thoughtful, challenging materials that develop students' learning, they offer meaningful learning experiences in which students learn and explore. Centers should not be just for fun experiences or time fillers but for learning experiences based on targeted standards that are designed to meet the needs of a variety of different learners. They are also great vehicles for offering students opportunities to use their various multiple intelligences. Figure 6.7, "Multiple Intelligence Suggestions for Centers and Projects," gives ample suggestions for centers and projects.

PROJECTS FOR DIFFERENTIATED CLASSROOMS

What Are They?

A project is an in-depth study. Students explore a topic as investigators, researchers, and discoverers of knowledge. Projects can be varied and rich with opportunities for engaging learners and for deep understanding at a variety of levels of readiness, interest, or learning profile. Projects are usually in a certain subject area dealing with a particular topic of study.

Structured Projects

In structured projects, the expectations and guidelines are structured and are shared with the students. Students work creatively to achieve success, given their understanding of concepts and the skills they have mastered. For example, in Geometry, students are assigned the "Building Project" (Build the tallest structure that will stand alone using the materials given). The project may be assigned to the whole class but responded to individually or in small groups.

Topic-Related Projects

These projects are typical, traditional school projects. Students choose a topic that interests and motivates them and produce a product that shows what has been learned or what is particularly significant to the learners. For example, students choose a political figure, an issue, or a particular place or event associated with World War II that interests them.

Open-Ended Projects

These projects have minimal guidelines, few criteria, and are loosely structured to encourage risk taking and creativity. These projects may be a challenge that causes students to draw on their knowledge and skills to produce a product that addresses the challenge. One middle school class looked at developing innovative products that would be useful to the elderly. The

Figure 6.7. Multiple Intelligences: Suggestions for Centers and Projects

Verbal/Linguistic
Prepare a report
Write a play or essay
Create a poem or recitation
Listen to an audiotape on . . .
Interview
Label a diagram
Give directions for . . .

Bodily/Kinesthetic
Create a role-play
Construct a model
    or representation
Develop a mime
Create a tableau for . . .
Manipulate materials
Work through a simulation
Create actions for . . .

Musical/Rhythmic
Compose a rap song or rhyme
Create a jingle to teach others . . .
Listen to musical selections about . . .
Write a poem
Select music or songs
    for a particular purpose

Naturalist
Discover or experiment
Categorize materials or ideas
Look for ideas from nature
Adapt materials to a new use
Connect ideas to nature
Examine materials
    to make generalizations

Visual/Spatial
Draw a picture
Create a mural or display
Illustrate an event
Make a diagram
Create a cartoon
Paint or design a poster
Design a graphic
Use color to . . .

Interpersonal
Work with a partner or group
Discuss and come
    to conclusions
Solve a problem together
Survey or interview others
Dialogue about a topic
Use cooperative groups

Logical/Mathematical
Create a pattern
Describe a sequence or process
Develop a rationale
Analyze a situation
Critically assess . . .
Classify, rank, or compare . . .
Interpret evidence . . .

Intrapersonal
Think about and plan
Write in a journal
Review or visualize a way
    to do something
Make a connection with
    past information or experiences
Metacognitive moments

unit contained literacy skills as students developed questionnaires, surveys, and interviews to gather data from the elderly. They used the Internet to access information on trends and needs. They used principles of simple machines and other science and math skills. In a hands-on and creative component they designed their invention.

Why Do We Use Them?

Projects are used because they build on students' interest and satisfy curiosity. Students learn to plan their time and develop their research skills at various levels. Projects provide students with choices, ownership, and responsibility. They encourage independence and self-directed learning skills and allow students to work at complex and abstract levels that match their skill level while managing time and materials. Projects are highly motivating and allow for in-depth work on interesting topics. Projects allow students to work at their own rate. However, they must be worth the academic time of the learner and be meaningful experiences, not just time fillers. Projects help the learner to interact with knowledge at a level higher than simple recall. They also help develop concepts more fully and enable students to construct their own understanding. Information learned in context with an emotional hook will be remembered longer if it is also a meaningful experience. Projects emphasize process as well as product and integrate many concepts, facts, and skills.

How Do We Use Them?

All projects need to be designed with the end in mind. That means the project is designed based on clear learning goals, standards, and content objectives. Projects should be age appropriate and at the students' level so the work is interesting and challenging without being overwhelming.

Suggestion List

Teachers usually provide students with a suggestion list for projects. Design the list with a variety of intelligences targeted both so that the learners can work on an area of strength for the presentation and format and because students' learning styles are diverse (see Figure 2.10, "Suggestions for Using the 8 Intelligences," or Figure 6.7, "Multiple Intelligences: Suggestions for Centers and Projects"). This allows learners to concentrate on information and spend time on developing comprehension and a deeper understanding of the topic rather than always having to use verbal linguistic models like essays, research papers, or oral presentations.

The following is an example of nutrition project choices that teacher Cindy Palur (Granville, OH) designed to consciously offer options in the area of Multiple Intelligences:

Action Project Ideas for Nutrition Class

If you are musical or rhythmic, you might like to

♦ Compose a song related to wellness

♦ Create a nutritional poem

♦ Make up a health-related rap song

If you like to write or talk, you might like to

♦ Write memos to be announced each morning to improve student wellness

♦ Create a nutritional commercial

♦ Write a report related to a wellness issue

♦ Create a nutritional brochure

♦ Read a nutritional or health-related book and make a report

♦ Interview a health professional and report your findings

♦ Keep a daily journal of your eating and exercise for a week and report on how they can be improved

If you like to dance or perform, you might like to

♦ Perform a play, dance, or skit depicting various elements of nutrition (eating disorders, coronary disease, etc.)

♦ Make a complete dinner for friends or family

♦ Create a routine or jazzercise dance to your favorite song and teach it to several friends.

♦ Compose a poem or make a tape or video of an element related to wellness

If you like to work with others, you might like to

♦ Volunteer at a food pantry or soup kitchen

♦ Volunteer to help a caterer

♦ Survey people who work in some aspect of nutrition and help them make positive changes to improve their level of wellness. Keep in touch as to their progress (e.g., set up an exercise or low-fat eating program)

♦ Organize an exercise or workout group and meet regularly

♦ Teach an elementary class an aspect of nutrition (e.g., "5 a Day")

If you like to use numbers or graphs or solve abstract problems, you might like to

♦ Collect data to make a graph to show the relationship of a health issue (e.g., Is there a relationship between students who eat five fruits and vegetables a day and normal weight?)

♦ Develop a board game

♦ Do a science experiment related to food (amount of fat, sugar, salt, acid base, etc.)

♦ Determine how many calories you need each day based on your size and level of activity and create a menu to reflect that number of calories

♦ Use a computer to create a nutritional or health brochure

♦ Compare and contrast various nutritional information (e.g., water vs. sports drinks)

♦ Do research related to food

If you like independent study and self-improvement, you might like to

♦ Keep a diary of your diet for a week and determine ways you can improve to meet the requirements of the Food Pyramid and Dietary Guidelines

♦ Plan family meals for a week and create a shopping list

♦ Set wellness goals and ways to accomplish them (e.g., gain weight, lose weight, or exercise regularly); keep track of your progress

♦ Attend a wellness conference, seminar, or workshop and report your findings

If you like to draw or create, you might like to

♦ Draw a picture or poster depicting good nutrition for display in the cafeteria

♦ Create a new recipe and test it on friends or family

♦ Create an educational game around aspects of wellness or good nutrition

♦ Make a videotape showing good nutritional ideas

♦ Create new garnish ideas using food to entice young eaters to try new foods

♦ Draw an artistic wellness brochure

If you are into nature and growing things, you might like to

♦ Grow your own food and use it in a recipe (e.g., herbs)

♦ Freeze, can, dry, or preserve food for later use (frozen corn, canned tomatoes, applesauce, jelly, frozen broccoli, dried apples, etc.)

Procedure for Project Work

1. Choose a topic

2. Develop a plan of action that includes timeline, distribution of duties if working in a group, and so on

3. Implement the plan
   Gather ideas
   List resources
   Decide the format
   Refer to a rubric
   Conference
   Compile ideas
   Prepare presentation

4. Display and presentation

Evaluation: Self, Peer, Teacher, Significant Other

Students may be given the option to submit a contract for a project. This contract should meet the same criteria as the other suggested project assignments but would reflect the area of study chosen by the student. The student presents the contract to the teacher for approval. This is done best in a teacher/student conference so the learner can explain his or her thinking and ideas in detail. The teacher negotiates with the student until a reasonable contract is completed. Contracts may be proposed because the student has an interest in learning more about a particular area. This is important to learning because it satisfies the learner's personal learning needs. Students with a keen need and desire to learn will indeed learn more. They will be more committed and engaged and will invest more time and energy in the project.

Assessment

Rubrics are designed with clear criteria and indicators to establish expectations and the grading format. They include a detailed explanation of the requirements. Students should be clear up front about the criteria for success, and the rubric can guide them as they work on the project. The rubric informs the teacher, the student, and the parents about the requirements, guidelines, and expectations for the project from the beginning to the end (Figure 6.8).

Students log and journal their timelines, findings, and procedures to show what they are learning, using, and processing. If working with others, they need to negotiate the workload and facilitate the project by using appropriate social skills. Students also need to reflect on the group's interactions as they work together. Teachers assign or students select the roles and duties for which they will be accountable.

Adjustable Projects

The teacher provides a range of resources matching the readiness levels of the students. The materials should be multileveled and age appropriate. Adequate time must be spent on gathering and selecting the resources. Students select resources suitable for their projects and naturally select materials that are appropriate to their readiness level. Learners rarely choose materials that they can't read or understand. Thus projects are invariably adjusted as a matter of course because of the individuality of each student. A variety of multimedia and human resources can also be used for project work. The Internet and technology are valuable tools and should be considered for project work. They are intriguing and engaging for many learners and help develop the skills of accessing, gathering, and managing information.

Math teacher Ellen Wilken (Granville, OH) who wanted her students to really understand integers designed the following project choices:

> *Integer Project.* Demonstrate knowledge of integer operations $(+, -, \div, \times)$, by using one of the following projects:
>
> 1. Make an 8½" x 11" chart showing integer operation rules with examples.
>
> 2. Write a poem, newspaper article, or comic strip about integers.
>
> 3. Construct a 3D art object, puzzle, or game that uses integer computation.
>
> 4. Write and perform a live or videotaped play.

Figure 6.8. Rubric for Project

Name _____

Project_____

Date_____

Self_____

Peer_____

Teacher_____

Accuracy of Information

2_____3_____4_____5

Use of Visuals

2_____3_____4_____5

Completion

2_____3_____4_____5

Presentation

2_____3_____4_____5

Team Member Involvement

2_____3_____4_____5

Used Time Appropriately

2_____3_____4_____5

Comments:

5. Write and perform a song or jingle.

6. Interview someone outside the class about the person's understanding of integers. Record or videotape the responses.

7. Write an autobiography about your understanding of integer computation and how it will help you in future situations.

8. Show evidence of integers in nature by use of photography, samples, or drawings.

She reported that students were highly engaged as they worked on their choices alone or with a partner. They had a far greater understanding and ability to apply that understanding as a result of the project work.

PROBLEM-BASED LEARNING

What Is It?

Problem-based learning consists of providing students with ill structured problems that are open-ended and challenging. Students use information and processes in real-world situations to solve the problems. Problem-based learning as a curriculum choice gives students the opportunity to work on problems in a real-life scenario. These problems are loosely structured and have no single right answer. They require investigation of options and application of the content and processes that students are studying and practicing.

Why Do It?

Howard Gardner (1993) defines intelligence as the ability to solve problems, handle crises, and produce something of value for one's culture. The ability to problem-solve is an identified standard in most school districts. Students who learn only the facts may do well on *Jeopardy*, but the ability to access information and use it practically and creatively (Sternberg, 1996) is a worthier goal because it is useful throughout life. Problem-based learning provides the brain with conditions that intrigue and engage. It allows for creative opportunities that provide learners with the chance to use their skills and capabilities in a variety of ways, use a range of resources, and balance their choice of learning with the teacher-directed objectives.

How Do We Do It?

Steps in Problem Solving

- ◆ Clarify or identify the problem

- ◆ Draw on background knowledge and experience

- ◆ Begin with what you know

- ◆ Plan your own approach

- ◆ Work at your own pace

- ◆ Use creative solutions

Clarify the Problem

Through discussion and questioning, students identify the issues and home in on the essence of the problem. A problem statement is then articulated.

Identify Resources

Students need to examine resources, including information and processes that they know from past experiences. KND is a chart that may be helpful for organizing this information (see Stepien et al., 1993, and Fogarty, 1997). The K stands for "What do you KNOW about this problem?" The N stands for "What do you NEED to solve this problem?" And the D stands for "What will you DO to get what you need?" Some teachers add a fourth element: P for PLAN. Students can often generate the first three columns but cannot get organized enough to proceed with their investigation. Planning is a step that many students need to think about. A plan may be modified as new ideas and information come up, but it serves to help students get started on their problem solving.

What do we Know? What do we Need to know? What can we Do? Beginning Plan?

Accessing Information

Once students identify what they need to know, they can generate sources for that information or process. This gives them opportunities to use the Internet and other information accessing systems.

Generating Hypotheses

After all information is uncovered and collected, students generate hypotheses for solutions.

Selecting and Rationalizing Solutions

A solution that students think best fits the problem is presented with backup rationale.

Sometimes, teachers ask students to take on an authentic role in the problem and to present to a real audience. One teacher asked students to work in groups as travel agents to design a trip to their state capital. They were to highlight the historical/geographical features of the city/area and present their findings to parents with a rationale as to why the class should visit the capital. This problem engaged learners in various ways. They were motivated to take the trip and find out what would be interesting to visit and also to present that information to parents. The teacher had targeted the learning goals and then enticed the students to take ownership of the learning in a hands-on, practical way.

Secondary teacher Michael Bait asked the following of his physics students: "Construct an apparatus that can consistently project a steel ball to hit a target." He asked a group that needed a greater challenge to "hit a moving target."

A health education teacher presented the following to her students:

Group 1. As a sports nutritionist, create a menu plan for a week for a female athlete who weighs 130 pounds and is 5 feet, 5 inches tall and plays on a soccer team.

Group 2. As a diet expert, create a menu plan for a week for a 15-year-old boy who wants to build muscle and put on weight before football season.

Group 3. During the next week write down everything you eat and calculate the nutritional value as well as the caloric value. Use the computer program to help you.

She felt that these three groups of students would be challenged by these problems so she provided a variety of contexts that would suit each. The third group was allowed the limited computer access available in the classroom because they needed that support to manage the calculations. Her focus was on nutritional understanding and analysis, and she felt that the mathematical calculations would frustrate them and slow them down, thus losing their interest. Students were asked about their preferences before this assignment.

Posing problems with open-ended solutions is a great way to meet the learners where they are and engage them in accessing information and coming up with creative solutions. Problems are useful at any grade level and with almost any subject matter. They are adjustable for different levels of readiness, complexity, and abstractness. As with projects, the students seek their level of comfort and creativity and choose the "size that fits."

Inquiry, research, or independent study is another curricular model that engages students at their level and interest. The inquiry model in Figure 6.9 is a simple flow chart that helps teachers take students through the process, beginning with an exploratory phase to define the topic and build background experiences and knowledge. The next step is selecting a focus and posing a question that they wish to explore. They examine alternatives, consider and select the most appropriate one given their findings, and decide how to communicate their learning.

Contracts

Contracts (Berte, 1975; Knowles, 1985; Robbins et al., 2000; Tomlinson, 1998, 1999; Winebrenner, 1992) have often been used to allow students some flexibility and choice in their learning. Contracts have the potential for students to develop "flow," the state in which they are totally engaged in a challenging and motivating task that matches their skills and preferences.

Contracts allow learners to

♦ Be clear about expectations

♦ Use their multiple intelligence

♦ Take ownership of their learning

♦ Learn to manage time and task

When teachers set up a contract they need to consider the standards that will be targeted and the objectives in the subject content that will be embedded in the choices. Assessment tools, timelines, and clear expectations should be identified up front.

The example in Figure 6.10 offers students eight choices for a culminating activity for the unit on World War II, plus a wild card for students to design an optional activity to be finished during the unit at their own pace. Some class time would be given for conferencing with the teacher about choices and to gather resources. Students could also work on this project as a sponge activity whenever regular class work was completed. After students select one of the options, they fill in the contract form (Figure 6.11).

Some teachers use a double-duty log (see Figure 4.8) so students can keep track of time, process, and progress.

Another type of contract is one in which the teacher provides some core activities that all students will complete plus several options from which individual students can choose. An example is shown in Figure 6.12.

Teachers need to ask certain questions as they plan and design a contract. Consider Figure 6.13.

(Text continued on page 133)

Figure 6.9. Flow Chart for a Basic Inquiry Model

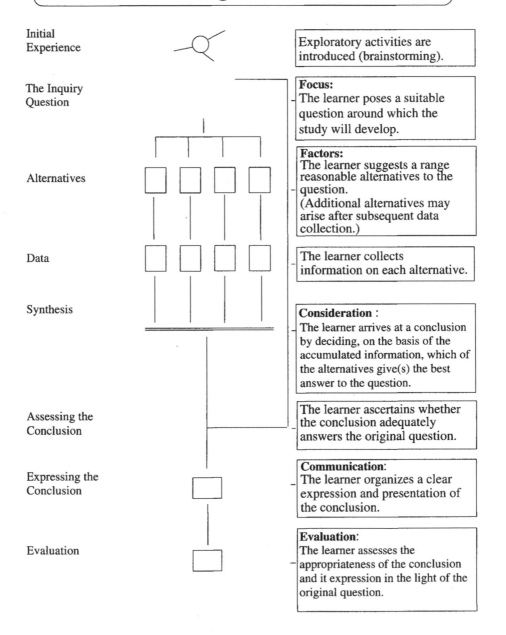

A BASIC INQUIRY MODEL

Initial Experience — Exploratory activities are introduced (brainstorming).

The Inquiry Question — **Focus:** The learner poses a suitable question around which the study will develop.

Alternatives — **Factors:** The learner suggests a range reasonable alternatives to the question. (Additional alternatives may arise after subsequent data collection.)

Data — The learner collects information on each alternative.

Synthesis — **Consideration :** The learner arrives at a conclusion by deciding, on the basis of the accumulated information, which of the alternatives give(s) the best answer to the question.

Assessing the Conclusion — The learner ascertains whether the conclusion adequately answers the original question.

Expressing the Conclusion — **Communication:** The learner organizes a clear expression and presentation of the conclusion.

Evaluation — **Evaluation:** The learner assesses the appropriateness of the conclusion and it expression in the light of the original question.

SOURCE: From Ministry of Education, Ontario, *Research Study Skills: Curriculum Ideas for Teachers* (Toronto: Ministry of Education, 1979, p. 20).

Figure 6.10. Example of Eight Choices Plus a Wild Card Offered Students for Study of WWII.

1	2	3
Design four posters using your own drawings or pictures that depict the characteristics of life during WW II. Use captions to explain your visuals .	Develop an interview questionnaire; then interview at least four people who lived in this area during WW II. Describe at last five ways the war affected their lives.	Write and present a short one-act play that depicts life during the war, either at home or overseas. Use support material from novels or historical references.
4	5	6
Read a book such as the *The Diary of Anne Frank* and briefly describe four scenarios from the story showing how WW II changed the characters' lives.	Wild Card! Your choice Please design an option and present it in writing by _____	Produce a PowerPoint presentation using visuals scripts and sound to present life as one would have experienced it during WW II.
7	8	9
Listen to a variety of songs, musicals, and film soundtracks composed during WW II. Referring to the content of the songs, describe what the music conveys about what life was like during the war.	Collect a variety of pictures, newspaper articles, photographs, poems, and stories, and noting aspects of life during WW II, create a personal diary of how you would have felt growing up in that time.	Create a board game designed to increase understanding of what life was like during WW II.

Figure 6.11. Contract Form for Student to Fill in After Choosing an Activity.

Name_____ Unit of study_____

I agree to complete the following activity: _____

I chose this option because_____

Please outline your plan: _____

_____

By the (date)_____
Signature_____

Figure 6.12. Contract Form in Which the Teacher Provides Some Core Activities

Author Study Contract

To help you improve your reading and writing you will complete the core activities and may choose any optional activities that total at least 40 points.

Please fill in the contract and hand it in by _____ .

Core Activities that everyone will do: (Points)

1. I will select and begin a book by _____ . (5)

2. I will create a "mindmap" character sketch about a main character in my book, (appearance, personality, friends/family, likes/dislikes). (10)

3. Each author uses languages in interesting ways. Select 3 passages that you think are unique and explain in your own words their meaning and why you think the author expressed himself or herself in this way. (10)

Optional selections:

4. I will write a dialogue that I could role-play about a situation or problem that I read. 1 page (10)

5. I will draw a story map or comic strip with captions outlining the plot. (10)

6. I will write a commercial, design a poster, or produce a brochure on the computer to advertise my book and/or the author. (5)

7. As a critic I will write an article sharing my thoughts about the story, outlining what I thought was Plus, Minus, and Interesting (De Bono). This will be a full page column. I will use the word processing program on the computer. (10)

8. Design an option and discuss with the teacher. (5 or 10)

This will give me _____ points.

Signed by Student _____

Signed by Teacher _____

Figure 6.13. Questions Teachers Need to Ask Themselves as They Plan and Design Contracts

What are the standards, content and skills that will be embedded in this contract? _____

How long will the contract last?_____

What types of activities will support the standards and interest diverse learners?_____

Brainstorm possibilities! _____

_____

What are the core activities that everyone will participate in?

_____

Should I design more than one contract considering the readiness of my students by examining the pre-assessment (simple to complex, concrete to abstract thinking)?_____

What weight should each task be assigned (points)?_____

All these curriculum approaches allow for adjustments in the learning, offer variety guided by the standards, and engage the learners with intriguing and thoughtful learning activities.

In our quest to find the "best fit" for our students we need to recognize that change is a process, not an event (Fullan, 1990) and that we are on a journey of continuous improvement.

> Teachers and schools should have a moral purpose, they say. But they present few ideas about what exactly the purposes should be. Going deeper means getting clear and coming clean about purposes. Not any purpose will do. Schools should reach for higher educational purposes that truly are moral in transforming children's lives and building a better world for the generations of the future. Among the many purposes of schooling, four stand out to us as having special moral value: to love and care, to serve, to empower and, of course, to learn. (Hargreaves & Fullan, 1998)

Educators need to celebrate how dedicated they are in meeting the needs of their students and how strategic teaching and learning have become.

The chart in Figure 6.14 offers questions for reflection by teachers as they move toward differentiated learning for their students.

Figure 6.14. Checklist of Questions for Teachers Planning Differentiated Learning for Their Students

Building safe environments

- o Do students feel safe to risk and experiment with ideas?
- o Do students feel included in the class and supported by others?
- o Are tasks challenging enough without undo or "dis" stress?
- o Is there an emotional "hook" for the learners?
- o Are there novel, unique and engaging activities to capture and sustain attention?
- o Are "unique brains" honored and provided for? (learning styles & multiple intelligences)

Recognizing and honoring diversity

- o Does the learning experience appeal to the learners' varied and multiple intelligences and learning styles?
- o May the students work collaboratively and independently?
- o May they 'show what they know' in a variety of ways?
- o Does the cultural background of the learners influence instruction?

Assessment

- o Are pre-assessments given to determine readiness?
- o Is there enough time to explore, understand and transfer the learning to long- term memory (grow dendrites)? Is there time to accomplish mastery?
- o Do they have opportunities for ongoing, "just in time" feedback?
- o Do they have time to revisit ideas and concepts to connect or extend them?
- o Is metacognitive time built into the learning process?
- o Do students use logs and journals for reflection and goal setting?

Instructional Strategies

- o Are the expectations clearly stated and understood by the learner?
- o Will the learning be relevant and useful to the learner?
- o Does the learning build on past experience or create a new experience?
- o Does the learning relate to their real world?
- o Are strategies developmentally appropriate and hands on?
- o Are the strategies varied to engage and sustain attention?
- o Are there opportunities for projects, creativity, problems and challenges?

Numerous Curriculum Approaches

- o Do students work alone, in pairs and in small groups?
- o Do students work in learning centers based on interest, need or choice?
- o Are some activities adjusted to provide appropriate levels of challenge?
- o Is pre-testing used to allow for compacting/enrichment.
- o Are problems, inquires and contracts considered?

Bibliography

Aronson, Elliot. (1978). *The jigsaw classroom*. Beverly Hills, CA: Sage.

Bellanca, J., & Fogarty, R. (1991). *Blueprints for thinking in the cooperative classroom*. Arlington Heights, IL: Skylight.

Bennett, Barrie, Rolheiser-Bennett, Carol, & Stevahn, Laurie. (1991). *Cooperative learning: Where heart meets mind*. Toronto, Ontario: Educational Connections.

Berte, N. (1975). *Individualizing education by learning contracts*. San Francisco: Jossey-Bass.

Bloom, B. S., et al. (1956). *Taxonomy of educational objectives. Handbook 1: Cognitive domain*. New York: David McKay.

Brooks, Jacqueline, & Brooks, Martin. (1993). *In search of understanding: The case for constructivist classrooms*. Alexandria, VA: Association for Supervision and Curriculum Development.

Burke, Kay. (1993). *The mindful school: How to assess authentic learning*. Arlington Heights, IL: IRI/Skylight.

Burke, K., Fogarty, R., & Belgrad, S. (1994). *The portfolio connection*. Arlington Heights, IL: Skylight.

Caine, Geoffrey, Caine, Renate Nummela, & Crowell, Sam. (1994). *Mindshifts: A brain-based process for restructuring schools and renewing education*. Tucson, AZ: Zephyr.

Caine, Renate Nummela, & Caine, Geoffrey. (1991). *Making connections: Teaching and the human brain*. Alexandria, VA: Association for Supervision and Curriculum Development.

Caine, Renate Nummela, & Caine, Geoffrey. (1994). *Making connections: Teaching and the human brain*. Reading, MA: Addison-Wesley.

Caine, Renate Nummela, & Caine, Geoffrey. (1997). *Education on the edge of possibility*. Alexandria, VA: Association for Supervision and Curriculum Development.

Campbell, Don. (1998). *The Mozart effect*. New York: Avon.

Cantelon, T. (1991a). *The first 4 weeks of cooperative learning, activities and materials*. Portland, OR: Prestige.

Cantelon, T. (1991b). *Structuring the classroom successfully for cooperative team learning*. Portland, OR: Prestige.

Cardoso, S. H. (2000). Our ancient laughing brain. *Cerebrum: The Dana Forum on Brain Science, 2*(4).

Chapman, C. (1993). *If the shoe fits: How to develop multiple intelligences in the classroom*. Palatine, IL: IRI/Skylight.

Chapman, C., & Freeman L. (1996). *Multiple intelligences centers and projects*. Arlington Heights, IL: SkyLight.

Chapman, C., & King, R. (2000). *Test success in the brain compatible classroom.* Tucson, AZ: Zephyr Press.

Clarke J., Wideman, R., & Eadie, S. (1990). *Together we learn.* Scarborough, Ontario: Prentice Hall.

Constructivist classroom. (1999). *Educational Leadership, 57*(3).

Costa, Arthur. (1995). *Outsmarting I.Q.: The emerging science of learnable intelligence.* Old Tappan, NJ: Free Press.

Cowan, G., & Cowan, E. (1980). *Writing.* New York: John Wiley.

Csikszentmhalyi, Mihaly (1990). *Flow: The psychology of optimal experience.* New York: Harper Collins.

Damasio, Antonio R. (1994). *Descartes' error.* New York: Putnam.

Deporter, B., Reardon, M., & Singer-Nourie, S. (1998). *Quantum teaching.* Boston: Allyn & Bacon.

Diamond, M. C. (1967). Extensive cortical depth measurements and neuron size increases in the cortex of environmentally enriched rats. *Journal of Comparative Neurology, 131,* 357-364.

Diamond, Marian, & Hopson, Janet. (1998). *Magic trees of the mind.* New York: Penguin.

Doyle, M., & Strauss, D. (1976). *How to make meetings work.* New York: Playboy.

Driscoll, M. E. (1994. April). *School community and teacher's work in urban settings: Identifying challenges to community in the school organization.* Paper presented at the annual meeting of the American Educational Research Association, New Orleans. (Available from New York University)

Dunn, Kenneth, & Dunn, Rita. (1992). *Bringing out the giftedness in your child.* New York: John Wiley.

Dunn, R., & Dunn, K. (1987). Dispelling outmoded beliefs about student learning. *Educational Leadership, 44*(6), 55-61.

Fogarty, R. (1998). *Problem-based learning & other curricular models for the multiple intelligences classroom.* Arlington Heights, IL: Skylight.

Fogarty, R., & Stoehr, J. (1995). *Integrating curricula with multiple intelligences: Teams, themes and threads.* Arlington Heights, IL: Skylight.

Fullan, M. (with Steigelbauer, S). (1991). *The new meaning of educational change.* New York: Teachers' College Press.

Gardner, Howard. (1983). *Frames of mind: The theory of multiple intelligences.* New York: Basic Books.

Gardner, Howard. (1993). *Multiple intelligences: The theory in practice.* New York: Basic Books.

Gibbs, Jeanne. (1995). *Tribes: A new way of learning and being together.* Santa Rosa, CA: Center Source.

Glasser, William. (1990). *The quality school.* New York: Harper & Row.

Goleman, Daniel. (1995). *Emotional intelligence.* New York: Bantam.

Goleman, Daniel. (1998). *Working with emotional intelligence.* New York: Bantam.

Green, E. J., Greenough, W. T., & Schlumpf, B. E. (1983). Effects of complex or isolated environments on cortical dendrites of middle-aged rats. *Brain Research, 264,* 233-240.

Gregorc, Anthony. (1982). *Inside styles; Beyond the basics.* Connecticut: Gregorc Associates.

Hanson, J. R., & Silver, H. F. (1978). *Learning styles and strategies.* Moorestown, NJ: Hanson Silver Strong.

Hargreaves, S., & Fullan, M. (1998). *What's worth fighting for out there?* New York: Teachers College Press.

Harmin, M. (1994). *Inspiring active learning.* Alexandria, VA: Association for Supervision and Curriculum Development.

Hart, Leslie A. (1998). *Human brain and human learning.* Kent, WA: Books for Educators.

Healy, Jane. (1992). *Endangered minds: Why our children don't think.* New York: Simon & Schuster.

Hill, S., & Hancock. J. (1993). *Reading and writing communities.* Armadale, Australia: Eleanor Curtin.

Hyerle, David. (1996). *Visual tools for constructing knowledge.* Alexandria, VA: Association for Supervision and Curriculum Development.

Jensen, Eric. (1996). *Completing the puzzle: The brain-based approach.* Del Mar, CA: Turning Points.

Jensen, Eric. (1998a). *Introduction to brain-compatible learning.* San Diego, CA: Brain Store.

Jensen, Eric. (1998b). *Teaching with the brain in mind.* Alexandria, VA: Association for Supervision and Curriculum Development.

Kagan, Spencer. (1992). *Cooperative learning.* San Clemente, CA: Kagan Publishing.

Knowles, M. (1986). *Using learning contracts.* San Francisco: Jossey-Bass.

Kolb, David. (1984). *Experiential learning: Experience as the source of learning and development.* Englewood Cliffs, NJ: Prentice Hall.

Kotulak, Ronald. (1996). *Inside the brain: Revolutionary discoveries of how the mind works.* Kansas City: Andrews & McMeely.

LeDoux, Joseph. (1996). *The emotional brain.* New York: Simon & Schuster. Lou, Y., Alorami, P. C., Spence, J. C., Paulsen, C., Chambers, B., & d'Apollonio, S. (1996). Within-class grouping: A meta-analysis. *Review of Educational Research, 66(4),* 423–458.

Lyman, F., & McTighe, J. (1988, April). Cueing thinking in the classroom: The promise of theory-embedded tools. *Educational Leadership,* p. 7.

Marzano, R. J., Pickering, D. J., & Pollack, J. E. (2000). *Classroom instruction that works.* Alexandria, VA: Association for Supervision and Curriculum Development.

Maslow, Abraham. (1954). *Motivation and Personality.* New York: Harper & Row.

Maslow, Abraham. (1968). *Toward a Psychology of Being.* New York: Van Nostrand Reinhold.

McCarthy, B. (1990). Using the 4MAT system to bring learning styles to schools. *Educational Leadership, 48*(2), 31-37.

McTighe, Jay. (1990). *Better thinking and learning.* Baltimore: Maryland State Department of Education.

Miller, G. (1956). The magical number seven, plus or minus two: Some limits on our capacity for processing information. *Psychological Review*, pp. 81-97.

Ogle, D. (1986). K-W-L: A teaching model that develops active reading of expository text. *Reading Teacher*, pp. 564-574.

O'Keefe, J., & Nadel, L. (1978). *The hippocampus as a cognitive map.* Oxford, UK: Clarendon.

Ornstein, R., & Thompson, R. (1984). *The amazing brain.* Boston: Houghton Mifflin.

Parry, Terence, & Gregory, Gayle. (1998). *Designing brain compatible learning.* Arlington Heights, IL: Skylight.

Pascal-Leon, J. (1980). Compounds, confounds, and models in developmental information processing: A reply to Trabasso and Foellinger. *Journal of Experimental Child Psychology*, pp. 18-40.

Personalized learning. (1998). *Educational Leadership, 57*(1).

Peterson, L. R., & Peterson. M. J. (1959). Short-term retention of individual verbal items. *Journal of Experimental Psychology, 58,* 193-198.

Pert, Candace B. (1998). *Molecules of emotion.* New York: Scribner.

Pinker, Steven, (1998). *How the mind works.* New York: Norton.

Reis, S., & Renzulli, J. (1992). Using curriculum compacting to challenge the above average. *Educational Leadership, 50*(2), 51-57.

Restak, Richard. (1993). *The brain has a mind of its own.* New York: Harmony.

Robbins, Pamela, Gregory, Gayle, & Herndon, Lynn. (2000). *Thinking inside the block schedule.* Thousand Oaks, CA: Corwin Press.

Rolheiser, C., Bower, B., & Stevahn, L. (2000). *The portfolio organizer.* Alexandra, VA: Association for Supervision and Curriculum Development.

Rowe, Mary Budd. (1988). Spring wait time: Slowing down may be a way of speeding up. *Educator*, p. 43.

Rozman, Deborah. (1998). Speech at Symposium on the Brain. Universtiy of California, Berkeley, March 1998.

Sapolsky, Robert M. (1998). *Why zebras don't get ulcers.* New York: Freeman.

Silver, H., Strong, R., & Perini, M. (2000). *So each may learn: Integrating learning styles and multiple intelligences.* Virginia: Association for Supervision and Curriculum Development.

Slavin, Robert E. (1994). *Cooperative learning: Theory, research, and practice.* Boston: Allyn-Bacon.

Sousa, David. (1999). *Teaching manual for how the brain learns.* Thousand Oaks, CA: Corwin Press.

Sprenger, Marilee. (1998). *Learning & memory: The brain in action.* Alexandria, VA: Association for Supervision and Curriculum Development. Stepien, W., Gallagher, S., & Workman, D. (1993). Problem-based learning for traditional and interdisciplinary classrooms. *Journal for Gifted Education 16* (4), 338-357.

Sternberg, Robert. (1996). *Successful intelligence: How practical and creative intelligence determine success in life.* New York: Simon & Schuster.

Stiggins, Richard. (1993). *Student centered classroom assessment.* Englewood Cliffs, NJ: Prentice Hall.

Sylwester, Robert. (1995). *A celebration of neurons: An educator's guide to the brain.* Alexandria, VA: Association for Supervision and Curriculum Development.

Tomlinson, C. A. (1998). *Differentiating instruction: Facilitator's guide.* Alexandria, VA: Association for Supervision and Curriculum Development.

Tomlinson, C. A. (1999). *The differentiated classroom: Responding to the needs of all learners.* Alexandria, VA: Association for Supervision and Curriculum Development.

Tomlinson, C. A. (2001). *How to differentiate instruction in mixed-ability classrooms, 2nd ed.* Alexandria, VA: Association for Supervision and Curriculum Development.

Wiggins, G., & McTighe, J. (1998). *Understanding by design.* Alexandria, VA: Association for Supervision and Curriculum Development.

Winebrenner, S. (1992). *Teaching gifted kids in the regular classroom.* Minneapolis, MN: Free Spirit.

Wolfe, Patricia. (2001). *Brain matters: Translating research into classroom practice.* Alexandria, VA: Association for Supervision and Curriculum Development.

Wolfe, Patricia, & Sorgen, Marny. (1990). *Mind, memory and learning: Implications for the classroom.* Napa, CA: Author.

Index

CORWIN
PRESS

The Corwin Press logo—a raven striding across an open book—represents the happy union of courage and learning. We are a professional-level publisher of books and journals for K-12 educators, and we are committed to creating and providing resources that embody these qualities. Corwin's motto is "Success for All Learners."